PRAISE FOR *T*

"*The Call to Courage* respond
leadership in these times of political divisiveness. It provides an in-depth analysis of the issues we're confronting, along with current and historical examples of leaders who have courageously protected the well-being of students, teachers, and democracy. The authors, both seasoned school district leaders, speak from experience, sharing their own struggles that called for courage. The book's pragmatic ideas for strategically reducing polarization while advancing justice will serve the field for years to come."

**—Linda Darling-Hammond, professor emeritus, Stanford University; president of the Learning Policy Institute**

"*The Call to Courage* is a timely and compelling guide for education leaders navigating the turbulent waters of deep ideological divisions affecting the United States today. In a landscape where the viability of public education is intertwined with the very fabric of democracy, the authors—experienced school superintendents—provide invaluable insights into the essential role of courage in leadership. By delving into the roots of courage, exploring personal stories, and addressing pivotal questions, this book empowers education leaders, families, and communities to confront divisive challenges in a productive, human-centered way, inspiring a collective commitment to nurturing courage in ourselves and our students."

**—Lu Young, executive director, UK Center for Next Generation Leadership; associate professor, educational leadership studies, University of Kentucky; past chair, Kentucky Board of Education; former district superintendent**

"*The Call to Courage* presents a clear-eyed picture of how anti-democratic movements are targeting public education and the principles underlying a multiracial democracy. Drawing on the experiences of two former superintendents who have championed educational equity, the book offers a hopeful vision for how we can all stand up and make a difference. It is essential reading for educational leaders, school board members, and parents concerned about the future of public education and our shared democracy."

**—John Rogers, professor of education, UCLA; director, UCLA Institute for Democracy, Education, and Access**

"This book serves as a powerful rallying cry in the face of escalating ideological divisions that threaten the very essence of our democratic society. It sheds light on the challenges educators face as they strive to uphold the values of education while confronting attempts to impose narrow beliefs and stifle diversity of thought. Through compelling narratives and insightful strategies, *The Call to Courage* urges parents, educators, students, and community leaders to unite and bravely confront the forces that seek to politicize education and undermine its democratic principles. It is a call to action, inspiring readers to stand up for justice, equity, and a robust democracy in the realm of education."

**—Shaun Nelms, director of the Center for Urban Education Success, University of Rochester; author of *Leading with Purpose: Empowering Others to Create Lasting Change***

"The book is highly readable, practical, and a much-needed call to action. *The Call to Courage* confronts all of us, whether in formal or informal leadership roles, with the need to counter the dysfunctional and polemic attacks on local schools and districts and to stand up for the core values of public education as being inclusive, equitable, and purposefully diverse.

"The authors are veteran superintendents who write thoughtfully and knowledgeably about keeping clear that public education is the DNA of an improving democracy through educating independent, knowledgeable, and open-minded citizens.

"What sets this book apart from others about education and democracy are its numerous examples of how parents, librarians, teachers, school board members, official school leaders, and community members—through calm determination and activism—have reinvigorated education in their communities to be aligned with core values. Among the book's strengths are practical guidelines and procedures for countering hostilities, intimidations, and power takeovers.

"These two authors know of what they write from their challenges, their vulnerabilities, and their willingness to challenge the vocal and disruptive minority who strive for the demise of public purpose."

—**Carl Glickman, professor emeritus of education, University of Georgia; coauthor of** *The Essential Renewal of America's Schools*

"*The Call to Courage* is such an important work because it reminds all those who care deeply about the education and well-being of young people that we really can make a difference. Through examples of everyday heroes who have transcended fear to make a difference, the book inspires us to engage, offers us practical strategies for overcoming hate, and reminds us that courage is the essential foundation upon which meaningful action is built."

—**Brent McKim, president, National Council of Urban Education Associations; president, Jefferson County Teachers Association, Louisville, Kentucky**

"*The Call to Courage* is the right book for these times. Authored by seasoned practitioners and staunch advocates for public education and for children, it confronts the profound challenges posed by ideological divisions currently gripping our nation. Through compelling personal stories and insightful reflections, it urges educators, parents, and leaders to summon the courage required to champion justice and equity in education for all children. What sets *The Call to Courage* apart is its important message that courage is not only an innate trait but a quality that can be nurtured and developed with intentionality. This book is an inspirational call to action, and it's essential reading for those dedicated to shaping a brighter future for our children and our nation. I hope we will all join the authors in their call to courage, because this is a book that will inspire, challenge, and empower us to make a difference!"

**—Aaron C. Spence, superintendent,
Loudoun County Public Schools, Virginia**

"In its resounding message, *The Call to Courage* fiercely champions equity in education, promoting unity against divisive forces that imperil inclusivity and opportunity. Its riveting narratives and actionable guidance summon parents, educators, and leaders to forge an unbreakable alliance, fortifying education's pivotal role in fostering diversity, equity, and the triumphant growth of every student within our democratic tapestry. A vital arsenal for systems leaders and equity warriors alike!"

**—Alex Marrero, superintendent,
Denver Public Schools; president-elect, Association of
Latino Administrators and Superintendents**

"Our public school system is the backbone of our democracy. It is what inspires the true American dream for many of our students and parents, one that ensures a free and appropriate public education for all that leads to future pathways to define one's success. *The Call to Courage* is a must-read for those fighting to ensure our public school system continues to be that pathway for our students and families. Education has always been political, but never so partisan. This book explores avenues to support ALL our students, educators, and families on their journey toward acceptance in an ever-changing America."

—Gustavo Balderas, superintendent, Beaverton School District, Oregon; president-elect, AASA, The School Superintendents Association; president, Association of Latino Administrators and Superintendents

"Sheldon Berman and Luvelle Brown have written a book that is essential reading for school system leaders and parent leaders. As our nation wrestles with increased political divisions and as educators are under attack, Berman and Brown offer a compelling argument and practical considerations for leaders to defend public education. Courage is required if educators and parents are going to counteract those who want to tear down public education. This book will inspire and sustain leaders who want to do the right thing, even when it is difficult."

—Joshua P. Starr, managing partner, Center for Model Schools; former superintendent; former CEO of Phi Delta Kappa International

"I work every day with superintendents and other school leaders who are under attack—often, confoundingly, because they are choosing to do what is right for *all* students. Sheldon Berman and Luvelle Brown have written a book that provides a thoughtful and principled perspective about the importance of leading with courage in our divided communities, supported by personal stories that illuminate the difficult choices K–12 leaders face. Ready to stand up for public education and our democracy? Then *The Call to Courage* is for you."

—Craig Hawkins, executive director, Coalition of Oregon School Administrators

"*The Call to Courage* offers a blueprint for cultivating the audacity to lead in today's political climate. This is a must-read for everyone committed to inclusive education through bold, visionary leadership."

—**Charles S. Dedrick, executive director, New York State Council of School Superintendents**

"This book could not come at a more critical time for our schools and the children they serve. From book bans to curriculum censorship to discrimination that forces out dedicated educators, America's schools are under attack by a barrage of false narratives. These attacks are part of an extremist political movement masquerading as education reform. Elected school board members, educators, parents, and students are being targeted and victimized. This book explains the impact of extremists and how educators and communities can come together to counter falsehoods with truths and protect the democratic principles in our schools that strive to create free thinkers and provide equitable access to education for each and every student in America."

—**Colt Gill, former director, Oregon Department of Education; former district superintendent**

"Too often it is forgotten that our country is only hundreds of years old and is a grand experiment in representative democracy. At this moment, we are experiencing a political and social crisis. *The Call to Courage* reminds us that this is not a new experience for the country. We have worked our way through previous crises because people of courage have stepped up.

"In *The Call to Courage*, we read the stories of how positional leaders and ordinary people showed courage in times of need. The book is centered around equity as a core principle of democracy. While focused on education, it has lessons that reach beyond schools and schooling. In my own quest to understand the times,

I was buoyed by hearing the stories of how others chose to show courage, reclaim the narrative, and work collaboratively through open dialogue to resolve differences.

"I thank the authors for their courageous service to the field of education and for sharing the lessons they have learned—especially that each of us must lead from where we are."

—**Janice E. Jackson, former deputy superintendent, Boston Public Schools; former deputy assistant secretary, U.S. Department of Education–Office of Elementary and Secondary Education**

"When I was a very young boy, I remember seeing my parents' paperback copy of John F. Kennedy's *Profiles in Courage*. I read the book, appreciated the history, and didn't really connect to the lessons. As models who have stood in the arena, Shelley Berman and Luvelle Brown breathe life and meaning into those lessons through their stories. They help us understand the courage needed to go from vision to service."

—**Mort Sherman, senior associate executive director, Leadership Network, AASA, The School Superintendents Association; former superintendent**

# THE CALL TO COURAGE

# THE CALL TO COURAGE

*Standing Up and Speaking Out Against the Assault on Democracy, Educators, and Students in America's Schools*

SHELDON BERMAN & LUVELLE BROWN

THE SCHOOL SUPERINTENDENTS ASSOCIATION

ROWMAN & LITTLEFIELD
*Lanham • Boulder • New York • London*

Published by Rowman & Littlefield
An imprint of The Rowman & Littlefield Publishing Group, Inc.
4501 Forbes Boulevard, Suite 200, Lanham, Maryland 20706
www.rowman.com

86-90 Paul Street, London EC2A 4NE

British Library Cataloguing in Publication Information Available

**Library of Congress Cataloging-in-Publication Data Available**
ISBN 1-5381-9675-5 (cloth)
ISBN 1-5381-9676-2 (paperback)
ISBN 1-5381-9677-9 (ebook)

♾™ The paper used in this publication meets the minimum requirements of American National Standard for Information Sciences—Permanence of Paper for Printed Library Materials, ANSI/NISO Z39.48-1992.

*To every educator, parent, community member, and student who has shown the courage to stand up and speak out for the best interests of all children and for a public education system dedicated to protecting America's democracy.*

# Contents

# ACKNOWLEDGMENTS

Superintendents, even former superintendents, are loath to enter the political arena unless there is a dire reason to do so. The situation we currently face meets that criterion. Yet what prompted us as authors to move beyond our usual conversations about educational practice and to instead speak about the courage to confront the political arena was the passionate encouragement and support of colleagues and friends. They expressed hope and confidence that this book would advance the positive work that so many people are doing in that troubling arena where politics and education are now overlapping.

We felt the pain of colleagues—superintendents as well as other dedicated educators—whose work has been compromised or who have lost their positions due to attacks from extremists. We watched as critical programs that support the success of students were being undermined by a politics of indoctrination. We felt compelled to write about these travesties and these dangers in the hope that we can give others the strength and courage to stand up and be heard. This book has not been easy to write. We have written it with some trepidation, but also with a sense of urgency and commitment to the children we have served and to the preservation of the democratic mission of public education.

We want to thank all the individuals we highlight in this book from superintendents Scott Menzel, Aaron Spence, and Julie Vitale to educators Amanda Jones and Katie Rinderle, and from parent leaders Monica La Combe and Darshan Smaaladen to students JJ Briscoe, Emily LaBar, and Keely Meadows, along with so many others who have demonstrated their strength and courage in the midst of trying and sometimes hostile circumstances. They have given us inspiration, hope, and assurance that together we can overcome the challenges we face and reclaim the narrative about what best serves our students.

We could not have initiated this work and maintained momentum to complete it without the encouragement and feedback of so many who viewed this book as a vital contribution. Among those individuals are the reviewers with whom we shared chapter drafts and who provided valuable insights that deepened our understanding and helped to refine the case we are making. They dedicated an extraordinary amount of time to reading the drafts and giving us critical feedback along the way. This group includes Colt Gill, retired director of the Oregon Department of Education and former superintendent; Joshua Starr, managing partner of the Center for Model Schools, former CEO for Phi Delta Kappa International, and former superintendent; Craig Hawkins, executive director of the Coalition of Oregon School Administrators; Susie Alldredge, former teacher and curriculum writer; Janice E. Jackson, former deputy superintendent of the Boston Public Schools and former deputy assistant superintendent with the United States Department of Education–Office of Elementary and Secondary Education; and Lu Young, University of Kentucky associate professor, past chair of the Kentucky Board of Education, and former superintendent. These individuals sustained us as we thought through each chapter, and they encouraged us to keep moving forward. We are deeply indebted to them for their suggestions and their assurance that this difficult and self-imposed task was worth doing. We also extend our gratitude to all those who read the complete draft of the book and offered their support for its message by way of their public endorsements.

We wish to thank AASA, and particularly its senior associate executive director Mort Sherman, for endorsing AASA's copublishing of the book and for supporting the authors throughout their writing of it. We are appreciative of the many students, caregivers, educators, and board members in the Ithaca City School District for supporting our efforts—not only to document the issues addressed in this book but also to work with others in the field to further their undertakings in areas such as social-emotional learning, equity, diversity, and inclusion. And we wish to acknowledge the professional kindness of Jay Goldman in granting us permission to incorporate into chapter 7 some of our writing that previously appeared in the School Administrator magazine, which he serves as editor.

We owe our deepest gratitude to our editor, Joyce Barnes. As a former special education teacher and administrator and now an exceptionally knowledgeable educator and writer, she refined and sharpened our focus and our writing so that we would be as clear, informative, and accurate as possible in the ideas we are delivering. Her dedication and commitment to ensuring that this book will make a difference stretched far beyond the role of any traditional editor. We thank her for working alongside us and for her passionate interest in the effectiveness of the book's message.

Writing a book inevitably consumes time that would otherwise be spent with family. We thank our families—particularly Sarah Haavind, Landyn Brown, Aiden Brown, and Bobby Brown—for their support, patience, and understanding as we devoted what must have seemed like endless hours to crafting and honing the book's content, tone, and import.

And finally, we thank you, the reader. By picking up this book, you are taking one more step to ensure that our children receive an education that teaches them to think independently and critically, to build bridges among people of difference, and to value the role of public education in a democratic society.

CHAPTER 1

# Courage Abides in Each of Us

*First they came for the socialists, and I did not speak out—because I was not a socialist. Then they came for the trade unionists, and I did not speak out—because I was not a trade unionist. Then they came for the Jews, and I did not speak out—because I was not a Jew. Then they came for me—and there was no one left to speak for me.*

—MARTIN NIEMÖLLER, GERMAN LUTHERAN PASTOR

THE UNITED STATES IS BEING ROCKED BY DEEP IDEOLOGICAL divisions that are significantly impacting the education and well-being of children. Sadly, these divisions are not new. However, the breadth of the current divisions appear sufficiently threatening that they may undermine the quality of public education and, by extension, our very democracy.

In this moment, the times and the circumstances call out for individuals to take the reins of leadership—not leadership equated with a person's title in an organization or position in a community, but leadership showing others the way to a goal, whether walking ahead of them or beside them. It means organizing, directing, setting in motion—steps that can be undertaken by any person with courage and commitment.

Standing up to the voices of division demands that education leaders, educators, and parents demonstrate courage. It means bringing a new set of skills to the problem in order to counterbalance these voices and to grow the understanding and support for democratic principles that underlie public education. That means holding firm to ethical principles, being willing to confront injustice and oppression, and accepting risks in order to make a difference for others—especially children and students.

But social justice and social progress, like personal growth, do not happen overnight. How have others who have faced divisive educational and political division dealt with the risks and discomfort of trying to heal human divisions? How do we as education leaders, educators, and parents dig deep into ourselves and find the courage to respond in ways that are effective, rather than shrink back or pretend to look the other way? How do we nurture the courage to remain committed to the long and difficult work ahead?

How do we help other parents, community members, and elected officials display the courage to assist schools in achieving their mission of strengthening democracy? And how do we as education leaders, educators, and parents support students in developing the courage they will need to persevere in the face of adversity, to make difficult decisions, and to seek and identify truth?

The authors of this book, as current and former school district superintendents who worked closely with educators and parents to overcome challenges and improve the well-being and academic success of students, asked ourselves these very questions. The search for answers led us to write this book. We started with the foundational concept that courage is not a mere genetic trait, such as height or hair color, something over which we have no control.

Instead, it is a personal quality we can develop with intentionality and practice.

But if courage can be learned, where do we learn it? Where are its roots? We began by looking inward, examining our own family histories, seeking the call and response in our ancestors' experiences that modeled courageous words and deeds. We consider it a privilege to share their stories with you here.

Luvelle Brown, superintendent of schools in Ithaca, New York:

Early each morning, while darkness still rules the sky, I peer intently into my bathroom mirror, taking a moment to reflect on my own reflection. Who is the person I see there? And what can he do, what will he do, to make the world a better place? And so begins another day.

Who am I? I am an ever-evolving manifestation of my elders' wildest dreams. I stand on the now-silent shoulders of greatness, strength, perseverance, humility, and love. As part of my daily reflections and writing, I note how much risk, courage, and love were displayed by generations of my family to provide me the privilege of voice and agency I know today. I do not take it for granted. I owe a debt to those who came before me—a debt I am honor-bound to pay.

I was reared in Central Virginia, the son of Bobby and Lucille Brown. My father was a truck driver and my mother served as a teaching assistant in our local public school. While my family did not have a lot of money, our community was tight-knit. My siblings and I received much love in that environment, as did the other young people growing up near us in a segregated part of Central Virginia. The level of patience, caring, forgiveness, and trust afforded us at home was abundant and affirming.

Unfortunately, that same type of love was not always available to us in school. Despite the love they received at home, many of my cousins and friends did not survive the supremacy culture and oppression that permeated schools. In order for me,

3

my twin brother, and others to make it through the system with our spirits intact, we had to muster a measure of courage that I've only recently been able to identify and articulate. Where did this courage come from? How was it developed in us? And how did it contribute to our survival?

Growing up, I was aware of the ongoing effort my parents devoted to rearing me and my siblings and the continual stream of sacrifices they made. Recognizing their excellent parenting skills, I often wondered aloud about their own parents and other family elders who must have supported their maturation and provided the love needed to overcome difficult circumstances. However, rarely were my questions answered with much detail or explanation of how we arrived at this place.

As an adult, tracking my family history has been challenging for many reasons, including coming up against the barriers of trauma and oppression that seem to have permeated my ancestors' lives. Folks died far too young from ailments brought on by generational hardships and stress. Other causes of deaths were unknown or, more accurately, not listed or mentioned for fear of the retribution that could be exacted if details were shared. Some stories of the dead were deemed best forgotten by the living.

But the need to know more about my family history still itched. In the summer of 2020, a friend offered support with genealogy research, and I unearthed details that shed light on my current identity. Most impactful was what I learned from the death certificate of my great-great-grandfather, Burton Payne. I found it amazing that I could be so moved by the few notations on this one piece of paper. Burton Payne was a man I had never met, yet without him I would not be walking this earth. His death certificate opened new doors, but left others firmly shut.

I discovered that he had been born in 1817 and died in 1922 at the remarkable age of 105, having worked as a farmer and lived in the same town for ninety years. I wondered about all he had seen in his long life, then realized that he had probably seen very little of the world. His father's name was not listed, nor was his mother's. However, in the space intended for his mother's birthplace were the handwritten words "slave of A. G. Willis."

It saddened me to reflect on the lives of this man and his mother who were responsible for my existence and that of so many other talented and successful people in my family. It is hard to fathom the number of hours, days, months, and years that Burton and his mother spent in harsh and untenable environments—working, suffering, sacrificing, surviving. Was Burton even allowed to spend his childhood and teenage years with his mother? Did he learn courage from her words and example? Did he wonder if his dreams of a better future for himself and his family would ever be seen with his own eyes? Did he nevertheless cling to the hope of what might be one day, and at some point was he able to turn those dreams into reality? His survival required a level of tenacity and courage that he surely struggled to understand or articulate. Yet that courage in the face of oppression was ever present and eventually pointed the way to greater access and opportunities for his descendants. I am one of many in his debt.

Fast forward to the mid-twentieth century, and my elders were still in the fight for access and opportunities for all. My mother's personal experience as a student in public schools had been anything but positive. Once a parent, those memories made her even more determined to change things for her children. She went to Board of Education and county Board of Supervisor meetings regularly for decades. At those public comment sessions, she spoke up on behalf of access and opportunity for all young people, particularly those who grew up in our part of the segregated South.

My father's experience with public schools had been similarly negative. He did not finish high school because he was not allowed to enroll at the quality school that others in his hometown attended—and because the segregated and underfunded schools in his rural community did not engage, educate, or tap into his many gifts and talents. Like other African Americans, he and my mother were keenly aware of the systems and policies designed to minimize their voice and opportunities. So they did what many folks did at that time—they used their voices to advocate change.

My parents' advocacy helped pave the way for access to an integrated high school that my older brother and sister would eventually attend—years after my parents had been turned away from that same site. Despite this significant success, the battle for equity and justice was not yet won. Day after day, microaggressions, racism, classism, and oppressive policies hit my siblings like a gut punch the instant they stepped into the school.

My parents realized that their work couldn't stop with opening the schoolhouse doors. They continued their advocacy so that the local children of traditionally marginalized communities would be granted not only physical access to the school building but access to all course offerings—including those typically reserved for the highest achieving students. Their actions taught me that courage must be heavily laced with perseverance.

You see, physical integration and assimilation were never their end goal. Far from it. My parents wanted the next generation of their family to feel that sense of pride and belonging . . . to know that they deserved to find themselves in the same challenging courses that had been traditionally reserved for their White counterparts in the now integrated schools. Because of their persistent advocacy, I was one of the first Black students in our school district to be placed in the illustrious gifted and talented program and ultimately was the first to take an AP course at the high school.

Yet my pride was muted. My experiences in those programs generated feelings of imposter syndrome. Acts of implicit and explicit bias made it clear to me that I was not welcome in this track with the school's highest academic achievers. Witnessing and recognizing my daily struggles, my parents continued their advocacy of systemic evolution. More meetings ensued, aimed at having young people from marginalized backgrounds (such as their son) be expected—and equitably supported—to achieve at a level comparable to that of other students in the public school programs.

While my parents' vision of academic equity and access for all was unambiguous and straightforward, the path to achieving it was circuitous and replete with obstacles. Walking that path in the face of unknowns demanded significant courage. Today, my nieces, nephews, and cousins attend school in a community where more and more each day they are known, seen, heard, and expected to achieve at the highest levels. Though long delayed, these are welcome and tangible signs of progress. The work goes on.

The sweat that comes from physical labor and the sweat that comes from psychological fear are two different animals. Burton Payne and his mother likely experienced both in large measure as part of their everyday existence. Since their era, the risks associated with my other elders' personal growth, learning, and continuous improvement also have been great. Yet even in the midst of oppression, my family found joy and achievement.

It is the same for me today as I give my full effort to lead a school district. The fear of retaliation, ridicule, bullying, and abuse associated with equal access and opportunities for all is still present for me and for others in school leadership positions who choose equity as a path. The disruption of board meetings, the passage of state laws forbidding conversations about race-related history and oppression, the sweeping book bans, and similar actions reveal that those who have for so long held the reins of power now feel threatened by the possibility—nay, the strong probability—that those who have been marginalized in our schools and communities will gain ever more voice and agency.

The challenges are many. School leaders who persist in the face of extreme resistance to social justice movements risk severe sanctions, including the loss of employment. As community leaders we must continue to show the way forward, finding inner peace in the knowledge that we stand on the unbowed shoulders of those who came before us. Yes, fear and risk have always accompanied us on this journey. That will not change. However, we must also ensure that joy and confidence are stalwart companions in our daily work. We must draw strength from the support of like-minded people, celebrating our achievements and even the smallest of victories. Together, in the pursuit of justice, we shall find the right path. The work is still underway, and courage is still the coin of the realm.

Sheldon Berman, retired superintendent of four districts:

"You! Behind the wall! Come out! Or we will shoot you right through it!"

Those were nearly the last words my father, a Polish Jew, ever heard. Because one woman faced down danger, he lived to see another dawn. Because one woman stood up to injustice, he had another chance to find the safe and normal life he dreamed of. Because of one woman's courage, he would someday make his way to America and have a son who would tell her story—and why her courage matters.

The dark and terrifying days of World War II reduced life to the ultimate struggle for survival. The small, rural town of Opole-Lubelskie in eastern Poland had been recast into a role it never sought—a transfer station for Jews plucked from their homes across Europe and now bound for Hitler's concentration camps. These Jews, officially destined for the death camps of Belzec and Sobibor, were confined along with the local Jewish community in an overcrowded ghetto surrounded by walls made of fencing and barbed wire. The local Jewish community was held responsible for overseeing the care of those in transit, even though already challenged themselves by the fear, hunger, pain, and indignity of ghetto life.

Without warning, on a frigid winter morning in 1942, German soldiers began rounding up all the Jews in the ghetto, including those who lived in the community, and herded them toward the train station. Among that number were my grandparents, longtime residents of Opole-Lubelskie. Knowing they were about to be forced to join the confused and frightened crowd lining up along the church wall at the center of town, they turned to their three children—all in their early twenties—and told them the end had come. Everyone knew that no one returned from the camps. There was no time for goodbyes. And then they were gone.

Hiding in a cramped attic space of their two-room house across the street from the church, the three young adults heard the shouts and gunfire as the soldiers marched the column of Jews, their voices paralyzed by shock and fear, toward the waiting trains and an unimaginable fate. The siblings knew their only chance to live was to somehow escape the abandoned ghetto and make their way to the countryside. But where could they find shelter and safe haven in a world gone mad?

For years, my grandfather had owned and operated a modest leather goods and shoe factory in town. Each of his three children was taught specific skills and entered the family business at an early age. My father and his brother mastered the craft of making shoes, and their sister was a capable seamstress. My father, a sociable and caring person, knew everyone in the community. Partly out of necessity and partly as an outgrowth of his personality, he often assumed the role of family emissary, trading leather goods and services for local farmers' eggs, milk, and produce. It was a fair exchange and people valued each other's skills.

Over time, my father became particularly close with one of the farm families who lived on the outskirts of town. They regarded each other as more than customers; they were friends who cared about each other's well-being. One day, several years prior to the war, my father was making his usual rounds and learned that the family was in the midst of a traumatic medical emergency.

The mother of the household had fallen seriously ill, and the local doctor said she needed surgery if she wanted to live. But where could this struggling family of farmers get the money for that kind of medical attention? Health insurance was nonexistent in pre-war Poland. The surgery, plus transportation to a hospital in the city of Lublin, would be prohibitively expensive. The family despaired of saving the mother's life.

Hearing of their plight, my father did not hesitate to step up and contribute as much of his personal savings as he could spare. When that amount still fell far short, he turned to other members of his family and asked them to chip in whatever they could. Through a combination of perseverance and persuasiveness, summoning the inner goodness of people, he raised the remainder of the needed funds. He then helped transport the farmer's wife to Lublin where she underwent a successful surgery and eventually resumed her life in the countryside. But that good and normal life was about to be threatened by a vicious war.

Back in the attic, the three siblings huddled in fear and whispered among themselves. During their time in the ghetto, my father had devised possible escape routes. On several occasions, he had tried a few of his ideas and was able to obtain a bit of food from sympathetic farmers—enough to help keep his family alive. But now there was no time left for a trial run. They needed a plan. They needed hope. They needed luck.

As hours went by and the sunlight faded, my father convinced his brother and sister that they might have a chance of surviving if they could reach his friends' farm. After darkness fell, with the town cleared of Jews and most of the soldiers headed toward their next grisly mission, the three Berman siblings crept out of the house and silently slipped through the streets. Though the farm was several miles outside of town, over the next few hours they found their way there, guided by their own memories of the roads and fields and aided by the hints of light emanating from the night sky.

Awakened and alarmed by a knock at the door, the farm family accepted the terrified young people into their home without question. No one had to mention the tremendous risk they were taking—not only with the Bermans' lives, but with their own. Over the next few days, they worked together to build a false wall, making a small space where the Bermans could hide and sleep during the daytime hours. Startled by every unexpected sound, the cold sweat of fear was their constant companion.

With all the Jews of the community gone, the newly vacant homes and lifetimes of possessions were being pillaged bit by bit. The farmer, a familiar person in the area, was able to blend in and unobtrusively remove three sewing machines from the Berman factory. As the weeks went by, this equipment contributed to the siblings' salvation—and to their downfall.

Hidden behind the false wall during the day, at night the Bermans stitched apparel, shoes, and other leather goods. These commodities were sold or traded within the town to help support the farm family and themselves. The new products, however, did not go unnoticed.

Antisemitism was common among the Polish people in the town and some colluded with their German occupiers. A neighbor had on several occasions observed the candles burning late at night, and he was aware of the leather and clothing products being sold by the farmer. As his curiosity turned to suspicion, he decided to act. One evening, after darkness fell, he crept closer to the farmhouse. Through the curtained windows, he glimpsed the Bermans at work and promptly reported his discovery to the local Polish police.

The next morning, four Polish police officers burst into the farmhouse, demanding that the illegally concealed Jews be surrendered to them. The frightened mother protested that she was all alone, that there was no one else in the house. Not believing her, the police searched the farmhouse and soon detected the newly constructed wall. Deducing that the Jews were behind that wall, they shouted, "You! Behind the wall! Come out! Or we will shoot you right through it!"

Wordlessly, the three young people exited their hiding place, expecting that every breath would be their last. They were lined up against the wall. The police captain gave the order for them to be marched outside and shot point-blank. Hearing those words, and without a moment's hesitation, the mother stepped between the Bermans and the police. Looking directly into the eyes of the captain, she announced with ice-cold firmness that if they were going to shoot the young people, they would have to shoot her first.

Stunned by the forcefulness of her statement and the courage of her stance, the captain relented. After ordering his men to confiscate everything of value that they could find on the Bermans's persons and in their hiding place, the captain agreed to let them go—with this warning: They must leave the area immediately; if found, they would be shot on sight.

But they didn't leave. Instead, the farmer and his family quickly built a new underground hiding place in the barn. There the Bermans remained sheltered for more than a year until the Russian army liberated the town and the three siblings could begin their search for the remnants of the life they had once known.

In an effort to protect himself from having to relive the pain of loss and suffering, my father kept this story buried deep within his own memories. Only after many years of silence did he begin opening up about his experiences during the Holocaust. Thereafter, when he spoke, this story was the one he shared most often. And every time he told it, present in his voice were the still-acute admiration and gratitude he felt for the courage that had saved his brother, his sister, and himself.

His words and his emotions seeped into my psyche. In recent years, his story has come to mind more often with the increasing incidence of antisemitism and of hate, violence, and mass shootings targeting marginalized or identifiable groups—Black, Hispanic, Asian, Muslim, Jewish, LGBTQ+, recent immigrants, and others—and the pressing need to build culturally and racially inclusive communities.

Not everyone has such a dramatic story in their family tree that reveals courage in such a profound way. Still, most people can think of an instance in which one person's courage made a difference in another's life. I know in my heart that I literally walk this earth today thanks to the physical and moral courage of a woman I never met. I can best pay her and so many like her back by paying it forward, by advocating the kind of social justice that has been denied to millions not only by the cruelty of war but by the inequities within our society and our culture.

As educators, parents, and school leaders, we touch tomorrow in everything we do. Although we may not always see the ripple effects of our work, baked into our roles is a responsibility to summon the courage to protect each other, our staff, our students, and our children from harmful words and deeds.

Like the generations of parents faced with segregated environments, each of us must speak up for equity in educational access and support for all students, regardless of race, ethnicity, disability, gender identity, or economic status. Like the farmer's wife in a land torn asunder by war and ideological strife, each of us must provide shelter, build walls between danger and the defenseless, and stand up to those who would tear down.

With gratitude to those who came before us and with abiding hope for those who will follow, each of us is called upon to lead. Entrusted with America's students, we must lead with a tenacious grip on our principles of fairness, with perseverance through times of struggle, and with the courage of our convictions, firm in the knowledge that we are creating a world that is more just for all. We offer this book not because we think of ourselves as examples of courage—although we have faced moments that called for courageous decisions—but because what we've seen tells us that courage abides within each of us, and that our current times call on all of us to find the courage within ourselves to stand up and reclaim the pursuit of justice, equity, and a meaningful democracy.

CHAPTER 2

# The Call to Courage

*We the People of the United States, in Order to form a more perfect Union, establish Justice, insure domestic Tranquility, provide for the common defense, promote the general Welfare, and secure the Blessings of Liberty to ourselves and our Poster- ity, do ordain and establish this Constitution for the United States of America.*
—PREAMBLE TO THE CONSTITUTION OF THE UNITED STATES OF AMERICA

THE IDEALS REPRESENTED IN THE FOUNDING DOCUMENTS OF the United States articulate a vision for the nation in which free- dom, personal well-being, fairness, and peace are attainable by all. Although the history of the United States, and of American schooling, is scarred by long-standing patterns of discrimination and the often painful quest for social equity, the vision of a dem- ocratic society that empowers its citizens to seek justice and the common good remains a constant.

Each generation has faced its own trials and fought its own battles in the effort to secure a more just union and extend civil rights and liberties to those who were disenfranchised. For some generations, such as those who confronted the challenges of totalitarianism in World War II, the struggle to sustain democracy was in response to attacks by enemies external to the nation; but more often the conflict emerged internally from division and dissension over who was deserving of specific civil and human rights. And every inch of progress had to be defended.

## FACING HISTORY

Despite the lofty vision expressed in the founding documents, since the nation was formed there has been a continual stream of people who walked the streets and fields and prairies of the United States while being openly demeaned, discriminated against, and disenfranchised: Indigenous peoples, individuals with disabilities, Irish and German immigrants, Catholics, Jews, Muslims, Chinese, Japanese, Vietnamese, LGBTQ+, Black, Brown. . . . And for some groups—Indigenous and Black people in particular—the mistreatment has been pervasive, unrelenting, and abhorrent. While the identities of the targeted sometimes changed, the unfair treatment persisted—all because their enfranchisement was perceived by some as an imminent threat to those who possessed status in society.

As televisions became commonplace in the post–World War II years, evidence of racial and political discrimination was on full display in America's living rooms. In the 1950s, Wisconsin Senator Joseph McCarthy led a brutal "anti-communist" campaign of political repression and persecution. Then, in the 1960s, the tensions over segregation and unrestrained racism divided the country even as the Civil Rights Movement pursued a vision of a more integrated, equitable society. Confronting McCarthyism, as it became known, plus deep-seated racism and other prejudicial ugliness, required exceptional courage from the country's leaders as well as from its everyday citizens.

## THE COURAGE TO CHALLENGE MCCARTHYISM

From 1950 to 1954, rabid McCarthyism tore at the nation as the Second Red Scare enveloped thousands who were accused of disloyalty to the United States. These individuals were ostracized, fired from employment, and sometimes jailed for their political beliefs. McCarthy led strident, accusatory, and baseless Senate hearings that attacked government officials, actors, writers, reporters, academics, labor union activists, and many others for their liberal political beliefs and their associations with liberal and left-leaning individuals and organizations. Many of these citizens faced exaggerated or false accusations as a result of their political beliefs rather than any disloyal activity.

McCarthy took advantage of concerns about the expansion of communist governments around the world to incite fear of and antagonism toward individuals whom he considered as leftists. The rampant McCarthyism led to loyalty oaths; anti-communist committees and loyalty review boards at the federal, state, and local levels; the blacklisting of individuals to prevent them from obtaining employment; state laws criminalizing communists; and the investigation and prosecution of persons suspected of communist collaboration.

The tentacles of McCarthyism spread to broader attacks on already marginalized persons, such as against individuals who were homosexual, accusing them of being a dangerous threat to state security. McCarthy and his proponents also pursued censorship of books and films that they accused of promoting Communism or being written by "pro-Communist" authors, even attacking the film *Robin Hood* for its Communist ideals. Not content to contain itself to anti-communism, McCarthyism extended to attacks on social welfare provisions of the New Deal programs and efforts to reduce inequalities in U.S. society.

Standing up against McCarthy and his campaign could result in an accusation of being a communist collaborator or sympathizer. It took the courage of fellow Senators, news reporters, activists, and students—as well as lawsuits that resulted in the Supreme Court's rejection of laws and actions sponsored by those supporting McCarthyism—to turn the tide. McCarthyism and its Second Red Scare damaged the lives of many and left a trail of fear, repression, and divisiveness in its wake. It exemplifies the consequences of reckless and unsubstantiated accusations and demagogic personal attacks on the character and patriotism of adversaries. It also stands as a lesson in how societal power can silence dissent and, equally important, how multipronged, organized dissent can bring about change in the arc toward justice.

## THE COURAGE TO MOVE CIVIL RIGHTS FORWARD

Confronting racial segregation, discrimination, disenfranchisement, and its embodiment in Jim Crow policies and laws in the late 1950s and 1960s also required enormous courage. Those advocating and working for the civil rights of Black people faced arrests for peaceful protest; attacks by police with fire hoses, billy clubs, and police dogs; and even death at the hands of segregationists. It took enormous courage for Claudette Colvin and Rosa Parks to refuse to give up their seats on a bus to White individuals. It took enormous courage in the face of antagonistic and harassing crowds and resistance from school and political officials for six-year-old Ruby Bridges to enter William Frantz Elementary School in New Orleans and for the Black high school students who became known as the Little Rock Nine to be the first Black students to enter Little Rock Central High School. It took enormous courage for four Black students to take seats at Woolworth's lunch counter in Greensboro, North Carolina, and for all those who participated in marches, voter registration drives, and Freedom Rides to claim the right of equality.

These individuals put their lives on the line, as did many who were not so fortunate as to survive. Reverend George Lee, Lamar Smith, and Herbert Lee, all from Mississippi, were murdered for their efforts to register Black people to vote. Herbert Lee was killed by a state legislator who was never arrested for the crime. Medgar Evers, an NAACP leader, was shot and killed by a sniper. The Sixteenth Street Church in Birmingham, Alabama, known for its civil rights organizing, was bombed, resulting in the deaths of four young girls—Addie Mae Collins, Denise McNair, Carole Robertson, and Cynthia Wesley. Civil rights workers James Earl Chaney, Andrew Goodman, and Michael Henry Schwerner were killed by members of the KKK for their efforts. Boston Reverend James Reeb was beaten to death for his participation in the march across the Edmund Pettus Bridge in Selma, Alabama. Vernon Dahmer, a Mississippi businessman, died when his home was fire-bombed for offering to pay the poll taxes for those who couldn't afford the fee. And these incidents only touch the surface of the tragedies that were intentionally visited upon those who died, were injured, or lost homes and employment as a result of their civil rights efforts.

At great sacrifice and with great courage, the Civil Rights Movement transformed civil rights in the United States, leading to the Civil Rights Act of 1964 and the Voting Rights Act of 1965. Although the nation still is confronting issues of racism and prejudice and state efforts to restrict voting in ways that primarily impact Black voters, the progress made in the Civil Rights Movement in the 1960s was a significant step forward. It stands as a model of courageous action in the face of significant resistance, intolerance, and threats of violence.

## OUR CURRENT DIVISIONS

During each of the generational challenges, there were individuals and groups who stood up against injustice, in spite of the isolation, ostracism, and threats to livelihood and even life. Sadly, we have again entered a period in America's democratic evolution when the courage to stand up for justice and for the rights of those who have been marginalized is required. The current culture wars in the United States have become extraordinarily divisive, and there is little meeting ground among those of differing political persuasions.

Tension between those who generally affiliate with one political party or another is so stark that it has created barriers among friends and even among family members. The resulting polarization has led not only to disagreement over policy issues but to a level of disrespect, abusiveness, and even vilification that borders on dehumanization of those with whom one disagrees. A Pew Research Center study (2022) found that "increasingly, Republicans and Democrats view not just the opposing party but also the people in that party in a negative light. Growing shares in each party now describe those in the other party as more closed-minded, dishonest, immoral and unintelligent than other Americans" (Doherty et al., 2022, p. 6).

At the same time, a significant portion of the population has rallied behind false conspiracy theories, lies about election fraud, and raw prejudice and hate. Some, who appear to exhibit a cult-like adherence to falsehoods, live in an alternate reality that makes engagement in constructive dialogue about differing perspectives nearly impossible. For others, the wishful belief in these falsehoods is fed by a fear that traditionally marginalized groups will replace the primacy of White people and White culture. More than a few subscribe to the zero-sum thinking that giving attention and advantages to one group will inevitably result in diminishing the lives of another. Some weaponize their prejudice and hate through false religious fervor echoing back to medieval religious intolerance. And for some, the opportunity to flaunt anger, prejudice, and hate and thereby deflect attention from their own inadequacies is bait they can't resist.

All of these motivations are amplified through an ideological war manufactured by political entities in order to secure voting power. Their success so far is due in large part to the inflammatory rhetoric and false claims they use to tap into the public's and parents' innately worst fear—that public schools are indoctrinating their children in attitudes and lifestyles that will undermine the values and beliefs that they themselves hold dear.

From the post–Civil War lynching of Black citizens in parts of the United States to the multinational support of or turning a blind eye to Jewish genocide during the Holocaust; and from prejudice against Muslims that emerged after the 9/11 deadly attacks on Americans and the symbols of American freedom to the storming of the Capitol building on January 6, 2021; and from the 1998 torture of gay university student Matthew Shepard to today's controversy over students' choice of personal pronouns—it is evident that overt and even covert displays of prejudice and hatred can generate mass appeal and response unless they are rigorously and broadly confronted.

In fact, incidents of hate toward marginalized persons have significantly increased across the United States, sometimes moving beyond hate to violence, as mass shootings targeting particular groups have become part of the daily news cycle. Some political leaders have fanned the flames of hatred through their rhetoric and public pronouncements, extending even to the floors of Congress. And some media outlets and social media handles have become propaganda machines for conspiracy theories, election lies, and disinformation aimed at promoting particular political perspectives.

When political leaders, organizations, and social media discount fact-checked news as fake; when they personally vilify those who take a counter position; when they discount scientific evidence, research findings, and data in favor of myths and prejudices; and when they promote lies and conspiracy theories, then the disparagement and disinformation are repeated and reported so often that it becomes challenging for many people to discern the "truth." This purposely generated confusion has contributed not only to mass shootings motivated by prejudice and hate but also to threats of harm to election workers and political leaders at local, state, and national levels.

In the modern news landscape, individuals can easily find partisan spaces that confirm their existing beliefs and prejudices, undisturbed by contrary information. This inability to distinguish facts and truth from lies, distortion, and exaggeration is likely to increase exponentially in the next decade as artificial intelligence enables more and more bad actors to create digital fiction that looks and sounds entirely plausible.

With the past decade's explosive expansion of social media and its almost addictive ability to capture hours of a person's attention each day, people are devoting significantly more time and energy interacting with the opinions of everyday people than hearing from experts in various fields. Social media influencers are paid based on the number of eyes they attract and the "likes" they receive. Some are financially motivated or supported by foreign nations to make shocking, misleading, and even blatantly untrue statements that people then share with friends, spreading the disinformation ever faster and further. With the decline of newspapers and the increase in streaming options, people no longer share an exposure to common news reporting that once helped shape the mindset of the nation.

While technology provides many opportunities for advancing the human condition, it is also easily manipulated to appeal to our basest instincts. This potential has been accentuated by highly partisan and siloed social media networks that promote cult adherence to myths, misinformation, and prejudices, rather than thoughtful consideration of scientific and research-based evidence and multiple perspectives on policy issues.

## EXTREMISM TARGETS PUBLIC EDUCATION

Against the backdrop of a divisive environment, and particularly among individuals with extremist views, this propaganda masquerading as news sows the seeds of authoritarianism as the best—and perhaps the only—route for winning against policies designed to cultivate equal access and opportunities for all. And those seeds are bearing fruit.

The past decade has witnessed a rise of authoritarianism in the positions and actions of political leaders in various states throughout the country. Governors have pursued policies and state legislators have passed legislation that undermine the voting rights and political power of marginalized groups; prevent educators from offering historically accurate accounts of U.S. history; promote prejudice against LGBTQ+ individuals, immigrants, and persons of particular nationalities or faiths; and impede the efforts of both public and private institutions and businesses to promote diversity, equity, and inclusion initiatives.

Most significantly, the extremism movement in the United States seeks to undermine public education and instead promote charter or private education, supported by tax-funded vouchers, where a particular political perspective can be perpetuated and where critical thinking about that perspective is not tolerated. As Hale (2021) points out in his thorough and historical analysis of school choice, the effort to privatize education and promote choice has deep racist roots and discriminatory results.

At its best, public education is an anathema to indoctrination and authoritarianism when public schools bring a wide range of perspectives into the classroom and teach students to think for themselves rather than to believe unquestioningly in the causes championed by particular political or religious leaders. A democratic and pluralistic society requires that individuals honor and respect differences in identities and beliefs, endorse the pursuit of truth through examination of factual evidence, and participate in open dialogue to resolve issues of difference. Education in a democratic society must support the development of these attitudes, skills, and values in young people. Yet our nation's current education culture wars are being fomented by those with extreme views who have an entirely different and contradictory vision for education in American society.

The general definition of an individual with extremist views is someone who believes in and supports ideas that most people find unreasonable and unacceptable—a definition lacking in specificity. For the purpose of clarity, the authors identify individuals with extremist views, a phrase used throughout this book, as those individuals and groups who support, advocate, and pursue policies and actions that are inconsistent with and undermine the concepts, processes, and goals of sustaining and enhancing a just, democratic, and pluralistic society.

The individuals with extremist views who are currently attacking public education are acting in ways that are antithetical to the goals of education in a democratic society. They seek to impose their own beliefs onto students and educational institutions through censorship of materials, perspectives, ideas, theories, and practices with which they disagree. They promote an intolerance of others through support for exclusionary and discriminatory policies and practices related to individuals of different gender, racial, ethnic, religious, national origin, or political identities. They advocate abandoning discussion or consideration of culture and identity—despite how important these factors are in promoting student success—so as to ensure the continued preference given to the dominant culture. And they close off inclusive and open dialogue as well as consideration of factual evidence, choosing instead to move forward with imposing their own agenda. In doing so, they politicize education, bring partisanship into the classroom, promote indoctrination, and undermine education's democratic goals.

People who hold extremist positions aren't necessarily explicit or truthful about their rationale or purposes. They often couch their actions in seemingly reasonable language to obfuscate their real intentions. For example, many of these people have adopted the catchphrase "parents' rights"—something that most parents view as appropriate—to advocate censorship of materials and viewpoints. In effect, this slogan has become a vehicle for a minority of parents to impose their will on the majority instead of conduct a dialogue about how parents can partner with schools to best support all students.

Another example of extremist advocacy is the effort to prevent race-based or ethnicity-based considerations and to remove any such provisions in current policy and practice, under the guise of treating everyone "equally." Although such arguments may on the surface sound sensible to some, they ignore the country's legacy of historical discrimination as well as current patterns of discrimination that impact individuals of color in our society. They reject treating everyone equitably in a way that each individual's or group's needs are met and instead advocate that everyone be treated the same, which has the effect of affirming and strengthening the prevailing culture.

Alternatively, some individuals with extremist views attempt to promote fear among parents by hyperbolic exaggeration, accusing liberals of placing pornographic books in school libraries and classrooms or saying that social-emotional learning promotes gender fluidity. Another strategy employed by these individuals is falsely accusing others of tactics they themselves are using, such as arguing that schools are indoctrinating students in the tenets of "woke" ideology when it is the extremists themselves who are encouraging states and districts to promote the indoctrination of students by advocating specific facets of right-wing ideology that are cloaked in faux patriotism and a sugarcoated version of American history. These tactics play on people's emotions, serve to confuse people about the truth, and portray individuals who disagree with extreme views as villains and enemies who are undermining the positive growth and development of children.

The preceding definition of extremism and the description of its followers' actions are admittedly blunt. However, the threats faced by public education and the attempts to use public schools as a tool for undermining democratic values are too real and too immediate to countenance more subtle wording. This chapter is meant to be a bracing wake-up call. The following chapters document dozens of examples of the extremist culture wars being waged in our schools today—and of the devastating impact they are having on our students and on the future of American democracy. This book is a clarion call to action in the face of these critical challenges.

## THE IMPACT OF POLITICIZATION

The impact of this politicization of public education has not only touched national and state policies but has descended to the level of local school boards. A UCLA study titled *The Conflict Campaign* found that in 2020 and 2021, nearly 900 school districts serving 18 million students were subjected to campaigns opposing critical race theory (Pollock & Rogers, 2022, p. 90).

School board meetings have at times become volatile with disruption, anger, and even threats against board members. During an eighteen-month period in 2021 and 2022, as noted in an investigative report by ProPublica, fifty-nine individuals were arrested or charged for acts involving threats or violence at school board meetings (Carr, May 13, 2023). Of those fifty-nine cases, charges were dropped in fifty-eight. As also reported by ProPublica,

> only one person who disrupted a meeting was given a jail sentence: a college student protesting in support of transgender rights. By contrast, almost all of the other individuals . . . railed against the adoption of mask mandates, the teaching of "divisive concepts" concerning racial inequality, and the availability of books with LGBTQ+ themes in school libraries. (Carr, May 20, 2023)[1]

In a growing number of cities and towns, individuals with deeply held political and sometimes extremist views get elected to public school boards, fire the superintendent, and then enact policies that censor materials, stop efforts to ensure a culturally responsive and inclusive environment, and prevent students from learning about history, current events, and even perspectives that don't align with those of the board.

Most educators, education leaders, and parents have not experienced this kind of politicization of education. We view education as the great resource for and bedrock of democracy, teaching students to think carefully and critically so that they can make sound, independent, and ethical judgments in their own lives and in their communities. When education is at its best, there is a profound respect for the consideration of multiple perspectives and generally a sense of neutrality on the part of educators. We definitely do take stands against racism, prejudice, and hate; but educators by and large avoid even the appearance of seeming to indoctrinate students in their own political perspectives. In fact, by its very nature and the diversity of its constituents, public education stands in opposition to indoctrination in particular political viewpoints.

Schools, with all their weaknesses and vulnerabilities, strive for adherence to high academic and ethical standards. Although most commercially purchased textbooks lean toward a conservative stance, educators, particularly in the field of social studies, have traditionally made a concerted effort to provide balance through the inclusion of multiple perspectives.

However, today's educators, education leaders, and parents are confronted with the misleading and inaccurate rhetoric of individuals with extremist views that public education espouses a far-left liberal bias and is intent upon indoctrinating students in liberal thinking. At the same time, they are grappling with a political environment and extremist advocates that are openly and forcefully trying to change education policy and practice in order to indoctrinate public school students in right-wing extremism and promote ethnocentric thinking.

The strident labeling and attacking of culturally inclusive education policies, social-emotional learning, and factual teaching about past injustices as "woke education" echo 1950s McCarthyism in their exclusionary rhetoric, personal vehemence, purge of policies that honor difference, and pitting of groups against each other.

At the same time, the elimination of diversity, equity, and inclusion programs; the attacks on critical race theory (CRT) and the idea of systemic racism; the state restrictions compromising minority voting; the attacks on gender identity; and the limitations on discussions of divisive concepts and social justice—especially those that focus on race—harken back to the rhetoric and actions of segregationists in the generations-long struggle for civil rights. All of these actions politicize and compromise children's education.

Bombarded with discriminatory language and activity, how should education leaders, educators, and parents respond, given their own professional and personal vulnerability? How should educational leaders address misinformation and maintain an instructional program that promotes critical and independent thinking? What stand should education leaders take when they are told to abandon practices that best serve students, or to censor perspectives that aren't aligned with those of particular political leaders, or to follow mandates that undermine their efforts to promote inclusive environments for all students? And how should they respond when individuals advocating those actions are in the audience at board meetings, elected to their school board, or hired as their new superintendent?

The response is the call to courage, the call to our deepest beliefs in the value of public education as the foundation for inclusivity and democracy, and the call to stand up for the best interests and well-being of our students and children. It is the call to find strength and resolve in the knowledge that this work is worth doing, this struggle is worth engaging in, and we are in it together.

# NOTE

1. This series was updated on June 5, 2023, to say that a second protestor, also a college student protesting in support of transgender rights, was tried on May 25, 2023, and received a jail sentence and fine.

# What Do We Stand For?

*[J]ust as a single candle can destroy a whole closetful of darkness, so a single life, lived in the light of goodness and moral courage, can make an enormous difference in overcoming the reverberating void that calls itself evil, blackness, doubt, cowardice, fright or mere bravado.*

—RUSHWORTH KIDDER (2005, P. 277)

*Living in fear is not living; it is tantamount to being a prisoner of our own weakness, constantly awaiting the next injustice.*

—GUS LEE (2006, P. 7)

EDUCATIONAL LEADERS, EDUCATORS, AND PARENTS ARE CALLED upon to make important and often difficult decisions on a daily basis. Yet we are more than simply managers of institutions, classrooms, and homes. We are ethical leaders within our settings and within the communities where we live and work. Our viewpoints and voices matter not only in deciding the direction to take in difficult situations but in clarifying and modeling for our children, our colleagues, and our communities who we are as leaders and what we stand for.

Rushworth Kidder, the founder of the Institute for Global Ethics, defines courage as a three-stranded braid that weaves together a commitment to moral principles, an awareness of the danger involved in supporting those principles, and a willing endurance of that danger (2005). *Merriam-Webster* defines courage as the "mental or moral strength to venture, persevere, and withstand danger, fear, or difficulty." The Latin root of courage—cor—means heart and in its earliest usage meant to speak from one's heart.

Courage, in essence, begins with knowing our heart and our moral strength—what we stand for, what principles and values we hold dear, and how we act on behalf of justice and care for others. The courage that we as educators and parents are now being called upon to display is not the daily backbone we exhibit in our handling of difficult organizational or interpersonal situations. With the politicization of education, we are being summoned to enter a broader civic arena in order to confront the current attacks on education, including policies that compromise the well-being of children, the instructional discretion to address critical but controversial topics, and the pursuit of equity in education.

## ENTERING THE ARENA

This arena is challenging for both educators and parents. Traditionally, we view ourselves as simply attempting to do our best to support children's growth and development; we're not especially comfortable with speaking out in the midst of controversy. In the current political climate, speaking out may mean becoming the focus of sometimes vicious and demeaning attacks on one's beliefs, practices, lifestyle, and livelihood—and even threats to the physical safety of one's self and family. This kind of attack can leave us vulnerable and wishing instead to be a bystander to the struggle. The offensiveness of these attacks is purposeful and actually meant to frighten people into avoidance, inaction, submission, and compliance.

Educators and parents, in general, tend toward conflict avoidance. We seek situations that support and affirm us and those around us. We move away from situations that demand us to address conflict—and political conflict in particular. In fact, educators are trained not to bring their politics into classrooms in order to honor the thoughts and beliefs of all students. Yet the current attacks on education seek to seriously undermine our children's well-being, the quality of education they receive, and America's future as a democratic society. We cannot afford to turn away from sights that distress us, nor can we remain politely quiet. These attacks will not dissipate on their own; they demand a response as well as continuing efforts at preventive initiatives.

Book bans; divisive concepts laws; attacks on diversity, equity and inclusion efforts; limitations on discussions of race and gender identity; the elimination of programs designed to support the social and emotional development of children; efforts to endorse specific religious beliefs within public school classrooms while disallowing others; and other antidemocratic proposals—the purpose of each of these actions is to ensure the primacy of a particular political and cultural perspective that is traditionally White, ultraconservative, monocultural, and sustained by compliance with authority. Children are viewed as the emergent tools to ensure that that culture and those in authority are not challenged.

To accomplish those objectives, any discussion or even acknowledgment of different viewpoints, past and current injustices, and differences in lifestyle choices have to be excluded from the school environment. In fact, according to that political and cultural perspective, classroom conversations about ethics, justice, and care on the one hand and the social and emotional development of children on the other hand have no place in the schoolhouse. Questioning and critical thinking are devalued in favor of rote learning a story of America that bears limited resemblance to the truth of our nation's history or the reality of our current society.

These initiatives and laws are detrimental to the development of students' social, emotional, and intellectual well-being, as well as their ability to think critically and independently. They are also inherently dangerous to a society and a country that value truth, justice, and democracy. They represent the seeds of authoritarianism. It is in understanding their clear and present danger that we can find the strength to stand up and challenge them.

## PROVIDING EQUITABLE, RESPONSIVE, AND INCLUSIVE SCHOOL ENVIRONMENTS

These policies and laws and the actions advocated by groups supporting them are dangerous to children's well-being because they go against all that we have learned from research on children's development. That research tells us that children's social, emotional, and cognitive growth are deeply intertwined and that compromising one negatively impacts the development of the others. Because these elements of growth are so interconnected, we cannot appoint the schools to be in charge of cognitive development while the home directs emotional growth and community programs cover the social aspects. Rather, in home, school, and community, children need caring and supportive environments that foster the emergence of social and emotional skills in order for their cognitive and intellectual abilities to thrive.

Overwhelming evidence demonstrates the value of social and emotional learning for success in school and life, as well as the constructive role that schools can play in supporting children's development (Berman, 2023; Greenberg, 2023). Eliminating age-appropriate programs designed to support the positive growth and maturation of social and emotional competencies undermines children's development academically as well as socially and emotionally.

Children also need to see their identities, cultures, and races reflected in the instructional and curricular materials they are using and to feel valued as part of their classroom and school community. We know that children do better academically when they feel known, valued, and respected and when they can identify with individuals of their same culture and race among the teachers, administrators, support staff, parent volunteers, and other valued members of the school community. Ensuring that our materials and our staffing reflect the many cultures represented in our classrooms is vital for the well-being and positive development of children.

It is equally essential that children interact with others who are different from themselves so that they learn to appreciate other cultures and are able to work and play well in diverse groups. Attacking efforts to promote cultural proficiency devalues and alienates those students who are from already marginalized groups in our society and compromises all students who can learn the benefits of diversity.

We also know that race and ethnicity matter and that each of us, even as professionals, has biases, prejudices, and a lack of knowledge or understanding that may impact how we treat others. Professional development in diversity, equity, and inclusion makes us more aware of our own biases, the kinds of actions and microaggressions that can unintentionally hurt others, and the bridges we can build across cultures. As adults, we can model these bridges for the diverse groups of students that are in every public school classroom. We can also become better attuned to institutional biases and practices that can negatively impact individuals of particular races and cultures, and we can strive to create more equitable, responsive, and inclusive environments.

Public schools must be identity-safe places, able to support the success of all students and provide the most productive work environment for staff—the essence of our equity work in schools. Ignoring race and ethnicity undermines our ability to create the kind of identity-safe spaces that are essential for students to perform at their best and for staff to be most effective. If we don't see and acknowledge the existence of race, then we won't recognize racism when it happens.

The same is true of our efforts to ensure safe spaces for adults and children of different gender identities. Our society has begun to acknowledge and include same-sex couples as well as individuals whose gender identity is not reflected in their sex assigned at birth. For too long, discrimination against and exclusion of these individuals have resulted in painful mental health issues, ostracism from family and community, self-harm, and suicide. Eliminating age-appropriate literature that includes same-sex couples and deals with gender identity issues—while presenting literature that projects heterosexual families as the only right choice—leads to social isolation, depression, harassment, and discrimination.

Schools have existing policies and practices in place for ensuring that instructional materials are age-appropriate, and teachers are trained to avoid inappropriate content. In addition, schools have existing processes by which parents can question particular materials and, in some cases, withdraw their child from specific content to which they object. However, schools also have a responsibility to accept and honor the identity choices of parents and students, both in the culture of the classroom and school and in the texts that students encounter. The added restrictions on discussions of history, race, and gender don't serve the purposes of ensuring materials are appropriate; rather, they stipulate a new definition of appropriate that excludes and diminishes other interpretations and promotes indoctrination in a set of beliefs rather than an openness to diverse beliefs.

It was not so long ago that schools denied their responsibility to serve children of other races or cultures and children with disabilities. With changes in attitudes and the passage of laws, schools finally welcomed these groups. Children with gender differences are the latest group to be devalued for something over which they have no control. Schools are one of the main places where such discriminatory attitudes can be turned around. Schools should be safe havens for every child. A child who is forced to endure others' nonacceptance may eventually turn that hate against themself or against the rest of the world; neither scenario leads to a happy ending.

Some persons who grew up in a largely segregated and homogenized society find that the growing diversity in ethnicities, races, cultures, languages, religions, and identities—and even the inclusion of persons with disabilities—is uncomfortable to deal with and difficult to accept. Many such individuals have long viewed the United States as a melting pot in which immigrants are expected to adopt fairly quickly the norms, beliefs, language, identities, and traditions of the dominant culture. Ill at ease around differences and untrained in appreciating the richness that variability offers, persons with limited cultural exposure feel threatened and double down on what they know and are comfortable with. As a result, these individuals support proposals and legislation that seek to impose their culture on others in an effort to create uniformity.

Although this behavior may be understandable to a degree, reflecting a fear of the unknown, it devalues all we can learn from human differences and all the richness that diversity offers to our society. This common tendency to insulate oneself from the unfamiliar makes it even more important to affirm that the role of schools is to teach students how to get along, how to learn and work with those who are different from themselves, and how to respect human rights and promote the human dignity of all.

As educators and parents, we also recognize that in order for children to learn, they need encouragement to take risks and they need support in growing from their mistakes. Adults who instead exert authority and force compliance—rather than offer empathy and understanding in response to a mistake, a violation of a rule or norm, or the expression of a different perspective—only stunt cognitive as well as social and emotional growth.

## NURTURING INDEPENDENT THINKING

All children need to become independent, critical thinkers. Success in work and life relies upon an individual's ability to carefully think through options, discern misleading and erroneous information, and make thoughtful decisions based on accurate information. Considering multiple perspectives, tolerating the ambiguity of not having a ready answer, and having the open-mindedness to reflect on one's own beliefs and understandings in order to identify errors in thinking are essential aspects of independent thought that will serve children well as they move toward adulthood.

To achieve that independence of thought, children require intellectual honesty. To hide the injustices of the past or cloak them with patriotic mythology does not help students understand the issues our society has confronted and how we have been able to make progress. Rather, such dishonesty inhibits students from learning how together we can make progress in overcoming the injustices and challenges that permeate our society and the world.

Our job as educators and parents is not to tell children what to think but to help them think for themselves. And the only way for them to develop that skill is for us to be honest about our country's history and current challenges; offer young people multiple perspectives on problems and solutions; provide them with access to data and scientific evidence; and teach them skills in critical and creative thinking, collaboration, and ethical decision-making. Just as we ask students to learn from their mistakes, we and they can learn from our country's problems and injustices through the centuries.

Efforts to limit discussion of race and divisive concepts and to create a distorted historical account only serve to diminish students' ability to think critically and make informed decisions.

When states such as Florida adopt African American history standards that distort and whitewash the horrific experience of slavery and direct teachers to instruct that "slaves developed skills which, in some instances, could be applied for their personal benefit" (Florida Department of Education, 2023, p. 6), and when the state of Florida approves as an educational vendor PragerU, a private right-wing organization that "offers a free alternative to the dominant left-wing ideology in culture, media, and education" (Schwartz, 2023), it is clear that the focus of these policies and laws is indoctrination in a particular political ideology, not critical and independent thought (Strauss, 2023). This state-endorsed behavior is an affront to all that public education stands for in a democracy.

Also foundational to respect for students' diversity and independence of thought is respect for their religious diversity. The secular orientation of schools is not the result of some plot to convert students to atheism, as some contend, but rather reflects a fundamental understanding of why the separation of church and state is so critical to democratic governance. We are a country of many religions and a country where individuals have the right to practice their religion; although it is important for students to learn about the various religions of the world, no one religion should be promoted over others in the schoolhouse.

The absence of religious practice in academic settings does not mean that schools and educators are devoid of ethics and values. Schools must have a strong set of values and beliefs grounded in respect for the dignity of all individuals and a desire for the common good of the community. Those principles are the essence of all religions—and of atheism. As U.S. Senator Sam Ervin from North Carolina once warned, "When religion controls government, political freedom dies, and when government controls religion, religious freedom perishes" (Ervin, 1985, as cited in Rabinove, 1988). The U.S. Constitution is a secular document with no mention of religion, and the first amendment in the Bill of Rights establishes the right to freedom from government interference in religious belief.

Supreme Court Justice Hugo Black expressed this sentiment with even greater clarity when he wrote in the *Engel v. Vitale* (1962) decision:

> By the time of the adoption of the Constitution, our history shows that there was widespread awareness among many Americans of the dangers of a union of Church and State. These people knew, some of them from bitter personal experience, that one of the greatest dangers to the freedom of the individual to worship in his own way lay in the Government's placing its official stamp of approval upon one particular kind of prayer or one particular form of religious services. . . . The First Amendment was added to the Constitution to stand as a guarantee that neither the power nor the prestige of the Federal Government would be used to control, support or influence the kinds of prayer the American people can say—that the people's religions must not be subjected to the pressures of government for change each time a new political administration is elected to office. (Engel v. Vitale, 370 U.S. 421 (1962))

The concept of separation of church and state applies not just to the federal government but to state and local governmental institutions, particularly schools. For the well-being of children's development, respecting the diversity of religions in schools is as critical as respecting the diversity of cultures and races. And it is equally critical that we not hold one religion or one culture above others as we educate children to take their place in a diverse and democratic society. Our focus needs to be on creating a society that is inclusive of the growing diversity of beliefs, cultures, and religions and that rises above sectarianism, instead emphasizing our common humanity.

## PRESERVING DEMOCRATIC GOVERNANCE

Beyond the impact on individual children's development, there is also a larger, societal reason for rejecting the policies and laws proposed to limit discussions of race, gender, and divisive issues; to ban books; to demean the efforts to promote diversity, equity, and inclusion; and to castigate a wide variety of initiatives that benefit children by labeling them as "woke," as if being aware of the injustices and challenges surrounding us somehow endangers our common culture. That larger reason for standing up against these laws and proposals is the very preservation of our democratic form of government. All of these monocultural efforts serve to undermine the very mission of public education—the promotion of democratic governance.

The foundational and ultimate goal of public education has always been to create a knowledgeable populace from whom and for whom a democracy can thrive. In his *Notes on the State of Virginia*, Thomas Jefferson articulated the profound need for public education in order to sustain the nation's democracy, writing to the Virginia legislature that:

> In every government on earth is some trace of human weakness, some germ of corruption, and degeneracy, which cunning will discover, and wickedness insensibly open, cultivate and improve. Every government degenerates when trusted to the rulers of the people alone. The people themselves therefore are its only safe depositories. And to render even them safe their minds must be improved to a certain degree. This indeed is not all that is necessary, though it be essentially necessary. An amendment of our constitution must come here in aid of public education. The influence over government must be shared among all people. (Jefferson, 1794, as cited in Butts, 1980, p. 55)

The fostering of civic development and engagement has been the core mission of education since its founding, echoed in the works of Horace Mann and many others in the early years of the

Republic. That mission is as critical today as it was then. The major difference is that our society is far more complex with a multitude of media sources that provide conflicting and sometimes highly inaccurate and misleading information.

To sustain our democracy, children need to learn not only to read, write, and do math but how to think carefully and critically. They need to be able to discern which sources of information are accurate and which are not. They need to be able to delve into the complexity of issues, hear multiple perspectives, and be open to being changed by those perspectives in order to make informed judgments. They need to have access to scientific evidence, research results, accurate historical information, and other data that enable them to separate fact from fiction, reality from myth, and truth from propaganda. They need to be able to recognize when dogma and doctrinaire rigidity prevent an openness to new or contradictory information. They need to be able to identify demagogues who offer false claims and promises and scapegoat others in order to gain popularity and power. And they need to be able to distinguish such demagogues from individuals who provide honest appraisal of issues, reject simplistic solutions to complex problems, respect and honor differences, and seek reasonable compromise among differing perspectives in order to advance the common good.

Young people also need to know about and talk about the "divisive" issues that are pressing for answers and solutions—and to consider alternatives. They need to be able to understand root causes and make judgments based on ethical considerations of what will serve our society and our democracy best in the long term. Depriving them of the opportunity to develop these skills not only compromises their ability to participate in government by the people but cripples our democracy and leaves us open to Jefferson's "human weakness." We must recognize that public education is much more than the process of acquiring knowledge and skills; it is an experience through which young people can come to accurately perceive themselves as having a meaningful role in constructing a better world.

Public schools are also the most significant place where children of all cultures, races, religions, and abilities gather and interact; where they can learn to respect and value the diversity among us; and where they can practice working and collaborating with individuals who are different from themselves. In providing these experiences, public schools also bring together the diversity of adults whose children attend these schools in support of all children's well-being and development. Although compromised by the growing privatization of schools through charters and vouchers, the public schools remain the one institution that brings us together as a society. As such, it stands as a bulwark of democracy. The undermining of public education, its diversity, and the pursuit of its civic mission opens the doors to divisiveness and authoritarianism.

Although the hydra-like attacks on education are being made through a wide range of proposals, policies, and laws that touch on race, gender, historical accuracy, and other topics, there is a core of neo-McCarthyism and ethnocentrism that runs through them all. It is an effort to erase the gains public schools have made in the areas of equity, inclusivity, and critical thinking, and to replace them with a brazen indoctrination in an exclusionary and extremist political ideology. The attacks present a false dichotomy that we have to choose whether schools will promote either right-wing or left-wing indoctrination when, in fact, public education in service of democracy should be the antithesis of indoctrination. The sole purpose of presenting this false dichotomy in this way is to open the doors to indoctrination in extremist political ideology.

So, the call to courage in this time is to reclaim and proclaim the value of the work that schools do to promote respect for diversity and inclusivity, to enhance the well-being and social and emotional development of all children, to affirm the goal for all of equitable access to education and equitable opportunity to succeed, and to provide students with the knowledge and skills that can sustain the future of our democratic society.

The courage to stand up is a personal journey. In pursuing that journey, we need to ask ourselves: How do we best serve all the children in our care? What is our vision of a healthy, inclusive, and respectful society? And what do we want our legacy to be for our children and our children's children? In answering these questions for ourselves, we can gain clarity on where we stand, which values we hold dear, and why we are advocating them. We also can be clear about the larger purpose of education in aspiring to and culminating in a democratic society.

# What's at Risk and Why Is It So Hard to Take the Risk?

*We must build dikes of courage to hold back the flood of fear.*
—MARTIN LUTHER KING JR. (2012, P. 120)

*Courage is being scared to death, but saddling up anyway.*
—JOHN WAYNE

TAKING COURAGEOUS ACTION IS NEVER EASY. As KIDDER (2005) points out, it involves an awareness of the personal and professional danger attached to taking a principled stand—and a willingness to endure that danger. At times in history such as the one we find ourselves living in today, it is not surprising that we feel uneasy about speaking out and stepping forward in the midst of controversy. A genuine sense of peril seems to hover over efforts to prevent education from being converted into indoctrination and to secure the well-being and positive education of our children.

**POLARIZATION GIVES RISE TO THREATS AND INTIMIDATION**
In recent years, we have seen the personal consequences suffered by individuals who took a stand and even by public servants simply trying to do their jobs. In the aftermath of false claims of election fraud related to the 2020 and 2022 voting process, election workers have been demeaned in public and their lives threatened and disrupted through anonymous emails and social media posts.

Perhaps the most notable case was that of Ruby Freeman and her daughter Shaye Freeman Moss, election workers in Georgia who were falsely accused of mishandling ballots in the 2020 election, and who testify that they now are afraid to say their own names in public. However, numerous election workers have been verbally assaulted and threatened in person, voicemails, and social media posts for simply fulfilling their sworn duties or affirming that there was not widespread fraud in the 2020 election. In addition, political leaders and their family members have been debased in social media and physically attacked.

Violence and the threat of violence have also become more pervasive. Domestic terrorism, particularly from right-wing extremists and White supremacy groups, is deemed a significant national threat.

The Anti-Defamation League (ADL), which studies extremist activity, reported in *Murder and Extremism in the United States in 2022* that right-wing extremists were responsible for 75 percent of the extremist-related killings between 2013 and 2022, with Islamist extremism responsible for 20 percent and left-wing extremism 4 percent. ADL's analysis further found that "right-wing extremists commit most extremist-related murders each year, but in 2022 such extremists committed all the murders COE [Center on Extremism] has been able to document" (2023, p. 8).

The ADL and the Bridging Divides Initiative also track threats to and harassment of local election, health, and education officials and evaluated over three thousand incidents between

January 1, 2020, and September 23, 2022. Their joint report found that approximately 30 percent of the incidents they reviewed related to education officials, that is, school board members, superintendents, and principals. The report concludes that:

> The findings in this report point to more than "incivility"—the data show a regular pattern of death threats, harassment, intimidation at officials' homes, and more. . . . Threats and harassment of local officials occur at a time when partisan rhetoric has grown increasingly strident and in some cases violent, and when many Americans may be disinclined to value democratic norms over partisan identity or policy preference. (Day et al., 2022, p. 25)

The actions of extremist groups, bolstered by threatening emails and voicemails from anonymous individuals, have increased fear and concern among public servants, including those working in education.

Other organizations found similar results. The National League of Cities conducted a survey in 2021 and found that 80 percent of the respondents reported receiving threats, harassment, and violence (Anthony et al., 2021). Locke and Luna (2023) conducted a study of threats and harassment experienced by all local elected officials in San Diego County and found such incidents "shockingly common." Their study surveyed all K–12 school boards in the county as well as the four community college boards, and all city councils, mayors, and boards of supervisors. They found that 90 percent of all the respondents had "either been threatened or harassed or have witnessed such abuse directed at their peers" (p. 5) and that two-thirds reported the threats had increased over time. They found that political polarization and the vilification of opponents were significant factors driving the threats. The study concludes that:

The rising volume and intensity of threats and harassment directed at local officeholders in San Diego and around the country undermines the legitimacy and efficiency of the local government and poses a major, if not existential, threat to all levels of U.S. government. If local political conversation between the public and their elected representatives is increasingly co-opted by political actors looking to disrupt and paralyze the political process, meaningful civil dialogue cannot be achieved, necessary public policies cannot be discussed sensibly, and faith in local government could falter. If, as our and other studies' findings have indicated, rising personal vitriol, producing increased anxiety and fear among local office holders, results in making people of good will, who are committed to the public good, reconsider—or withdraw from—public life, the void will be filled increasingly by ideologues and power-seekers advancing their own interests or that of a narrow segment of the community. This will directly and negatively impact the quality and professionalism of candidates for state and national office downstream. Local government serves as the training ground for politicians who go on to their state and national capitals. The stakes are high. (p. 31)

## SCHOOLS BOARDS POLITICIZED

As the national studies and the San Diego study indicate, acts of aggression have reached into the halls of public education. School board members have come face to face with angry, disruptive, and accusatory individuals and crowds whose threatening words and actions have caused some boards to end meetings and call on police to clear disruptive crowds from the meeting space. Some board members have experienced such angry and hateful messages that they have resigned their positions to protect themselves and their families.

The attacks come in many forms including doxing, swatting, front yard protests, social media attacks, vandalism, and threats to family members, in addition to face-to-face confrontation. Even posting a political opinion or a policy position on social media can draw vicious and hateful attacks from anonymous extremists. Although those who threaten and debase others are a small minority, the threat posed to individuals' emotional and physical safety and security is real.

The attacks became so numerous and extreme that in October 2021, the U.S. Department of Justice issued a memorandum of coordination authorizing law enforcement agencies to partner and intervene as needed. The department further issued a press release acknowledging the seriousness of the threats being experienced by school officials and teachers:

> Citing an increase in harassment, intimidation and threats of violence against school board members, teachers and workers in our nation's public schools, today Attorney General Merrick B. Garland directed the FBI and U.S. Attorneys' Offices to meet in the next 30 days with federal, state, Tribal, territorial and local law enforcement leaders to discuss strategies for addressing this disturbing trend. (U.S. Department of Justice, 2021, para. 1)

On the other hand, when individuals with extremist views are elected to school boards, they often take quick action to pursue their policy agenda and deter employees who disagree. In Woodland Park, Colorado, a group of far-right individuals were elected to the school board in November 2021. Once seated, they immediately began making significant changes. Without consulting any of the social studies teachers, they adopted the American Birthright social studies standards, developed by a right-wing advocacy group, that present a highly biased reinterpretation of U.S. history.

They approved a new charter school without public notice. They hired a new superintendent who agreed with their positions and forced out several employees who objected to the board's decisions. The new superintendent believed that the district should focus solely on academics and refused to reapply for grants that sustained fifteen counseling and social work positions in the district. The district also issued a gag order to prohibit employees from speaking to the media or posting on social media without the superintendent's permission.

In an email to a fellow board member, one member wrote, "This is the 'flood the zone' tactic, and the idea is if you advance on many fronts at the same time, then the enemy cannot fortify, defend, effectively counterattack at any one front. . . . Divide, scatter, conquer" (Goodwin, 2023, paras. 6–7). As a result of the chaos created by the new board, many teachers and administrators resigned, and parents moved their children to other districts.

In 2022 in Sarasota, Florida, at the first meeting of a newly elected conservative school board—with Bridget Ziegler, the founder of Moms for Liberty, as the new chair—the board fired the superintendent and began pursuing policy changes to reflect their own political ideology. Also in 2022, the newly elected school board in Berkeley County, South Carolina, fired the superintendent at its inaugural meeting and then voted to ban critical race theory as the first of many changes they planned to make.

Similar stories have played out in numerous districts as individuals with extremist positions have assumed power on school boards and led efforts to pass policies that support their political perspective. In 2023, in the rural school district of Crook County, Oregon, the superintendent newly honored as Oregon Superintendent of the Year resigned after her initial discussion with three "Mama Bears." All three women were associated with Moms for Liberty, had just been elected to a five-member school board, and made clear the directions they were intent on pursuing for the district. Dozens of states have passed legislation restricting the teaching of divisive concepts, race, and gender identity and many of the newly reconstituted school boards are moving forward to implement those restrictions.

## EDUCATORS TARGETED BY INDIVIDUALS WITH EXTREMIST VIEWS

It's not only superintendents and district leaders who have been directly impacted. Teachers have also come under scrutiny and attack. Karen Lauritzen was selected as Idaho's 2023 Teacher of the Year. In a matter of months, she found herself being attacked by conservative media outlets as a left-wing activist because she had expressed support for the LGBTQ+ community and Black Lives Matter in her personal social media, even though there was no evidence of her bringing those perspectives into the classroom. Parents in prior years had been strong supporters of her teaching, yet the negative and exaggerated comments in the media caused her current parents to question her everyday instructional decisions. As a result of these attacks on her character, within a year she left Idaho for a university teaching position in Illinois (Kopan, 2023).

Similarly, Willie Carver Jr., the 2022 Kentucky Teacher of the Year, was castigated in social media and at school board meetings for being an openly gay educator who was the faculty advisor for a student-led club that provided a safe space for LGBTQ+ individuals. The attacks were so personal and vicious that Carver left high school teaching entirely. Other educators recognized by the state Teachers of the Year program have experienced comparable attacks (Kopan, 2023).

In an effort to politicize the program, which is run by the Council of Chief State School Officers (CCSSO), some conservative states have changed the application questions from those in the CCSSO model. In Arkansas, the Department of Education altered one of the essay questions, instead asking teachers to write about how a recent bill instituting a voucher system and banning instruction about critical race theory, gender identity, or sexual orientation to younger students had a "positive impact . . . for Arkansas students." Georgia changed the application instructions to indicate that Teachers of the Year must refrain from voicing political views. Taking an opposing stance, Massachusetts added a criterion for candidates that they must be committed to racial equity, while California asked applicants to describe how their teaching supported state initiatives (Kopan, 2023).

Librarians in schools and public libraries have also been subjected to harsh attacks for resisting book bans. Amanda Jones, a school librarian in Livingston Parish, Louisiana, received death threats after she spoke against censorship at a public library board meeting and said, "Just because you don't want to read it or see it and [sic] does not give you the right to deny [it to] others." In reaction, one social media post directed at her stated, "We know where you work + live. . . . u have a LARGE target on ur back. Click. Click. . . . See you soon." And this was not the only threatening and vicious post. Others accused her of pushing pornography on children and grooming children—posts that terrified her (Smith, 2023, paras. 9–14).

Librarians across the country have been the target of comparable attacks. Schools in Tulsa, Oklahoma, received repeated bomb threats after the extremist group Libs of TikTok reposted a tongue-in-cheek video on TikTok by a librarian saying that "My radical liberal agenda is teaching kids to love books and be kind." It escalated further when Ryan Walters, the State Superintendent for Oklahoma, retweeted the video and added, "Woke ideology is real and I'm here to stop it." Similar bomb threats along with threatening messages were received in a library in Davis and a school in Oakland, both in California, after postings by Libs of TikTok (Derksen, 2023).

Even reading a book in class can have severe consequences. Katie Rinderle, a fifth-grade teacher in Cobb County, Georgia, was fired by the board of education in a split 3–2 vote along party lines. Those voting to terminate her employment contended that she violated Georgia law by reading aloud Scott Stuart's *My Shadow Is Purple*, a children's book about gender identity and the acceptance of all people. This new McCarthyism is targeted at intimidating and frightening people into submission and has resulted in librarians, teachers, and administrators leaving the profession to avoid the hateful messages, threats, false accusations, and demonization (Suliman, 2023).

## SCHOOLING MANIPULATED FOR INDOCTRINATION

Richard Corcoran, the former Florida Commissioner of Education and current Interim President at the New College of Florida, made it clear that education is the critical tool for moving a conservative agenda forward. In a 2021 speech at Hillsdale College, a conservative Christian college in Michigan, he said, "The war will be won in education. Education is our sword. That's our weapon. Our weapon is education" (Chait, 2023, para. 4).

Christopher Rufo, a key architect in the right-wing attack on education and now a Trustee on the New College of Florida board, was even more specific in describing this strategy. In a March 2021 tweet, he said:

> We have successfully frozen their brand—"Critical Race Theory"—into the public conversation and are steadily driving up negative perceptions. We will eventually turn it toxic, as we put all of the various cultural insanities under that brand category. The goal is to have the public read something crazy in the newspaper and immediately think "Critical Race Theory." We have decodified the term and will recodify it to annex the entire range of cultural constructions that are unpopular with Americans. (Beauchamp, 2023, subsection "The slippery Mr. Rufo")

In pursuit of that effort, extremist groups such as Moms for Liberty and Moms for America have organized campaigns across the country to take over once nonpartisan school board elections. Their efforts and those of like-minded groups have been generously funded by major donors and the Republican party. The strategy of indoctrination of children in conservative political ideology has become the new frontier in the culture wars.

PEN America, a nonprofit organization founded in 1922 to protect free expression through the advancement of literature and human rights, has been tracking state legislation, executive orders, and state or system regulations that restrict what teachers can teach about divisive concepts, race, and gender. As of November 1, 2023, they report that forty "education gag orders" have become law or policy in twenty-two states (Young et al., 2023). Taking a more expansive view of education legislation, Chait (2023) reports that between 2020 and 2023, twenty-eight states passed at least seventy-one bills restricting what teachers can teach about divisive concepts, race, and gender identity as well as what curricula their states' schools can use. Advocates of these laws and policies argue that they are necessary to prevent indoctrination, provide greater transparency for what is taught, allow families to have control over educational content, and shift the focus away from distractions to core academic content (Woo et al., 2023). However, PEN America explains that the impact of these restrictions is very different, in that they "silence ideas and identities that some find uncomfortable; control narratives about the past; and ensure that only one set of values, viewpoints, and ideologies makes it past the schoolhouse gate" (Young et al., 2023, introduction).

As divisive concepts laws were passed in state after state in 2021, PEN America sounded this alarm about the impact of these laws not only on teachers and students but on our democratic society:

> Their adoption demonstrates a disregard for academic freedom, liberal education, and the values of free speech and open inquiry that are enshrined in the First Amendment and that anchor a democratic society. Legislators who support these bills appear determined to use state power to exert ideological control over public educational institutions. Further, in seeking to silence race- or gender-based critiques of U.S. society and history that those behind them deem to be "divisive," these bills are likely to disproportionately affect the free speech rights of students,

educators, and trainers who are women, people of color, and LGBTQ+. The bills' vague and sweeping language means that they will be applied broadly and arbitrarily, threatening to effectively ban a wide swath of literature, curriculum, historical materials, and other media, and casting a chilling effect over how educators and educational institutions discharge their primary obligations. It must also be recognized that the movement behind these bills has brought a single-minded focus to bear on suppressing content and narratives by and about people of color specifically—something which cannot be separated from the role that race and racism still plays in our society and politics. As such, these bills not only pose a risk to the U.S. education system but also threaten to silence vital societal discourse on racism and sexism. (Friedman & Tager, 2021, introduction)

The impact has been dramatic on what teachers feel they can and cannot teach. The RAND Corporation completed two major studies to assess the impact of these laws and policies (Woo et al., 2022; Woo et al., 2023). RAND found that as of February 2022, one quarter of all K–12 public school teachers nationally were "directed by their school or district leaders to limit discussions about political and social issues in class" (Woo et al., 2023, p. 3). The study surveyed a representative sample of over 8,000 teachers and concluded that:

Not only are teachers having to seek ways to navigate this increasingly complex and contentious policy environment, but our data also suggest that limitations placed on how teachers can address contentious topics may be leading to consequences for teachers' working conditions and for student learning. Teachers described working in conditions filled with worry, anxiety, and even fear. They perceived that carrying out the core function of their roles—teaching students—has become more difficult, as restrictions on their classroom instruction limited their ability to engage students in learning, support students' critical thinking skills, and develop students' abilities to engage in perspective taking and empathy building. Especially concerning is the potential for these limitations and their politicized nature to lead teachers to consider leaving their jobs or the teaching profession altogether. (Woo et al., 2023, p. 23)

Rogers and Kahne (2022) surveyed a nationally representative sample of 682 high school principals and uncovered similar themes of stress, anxiety, and fear resulting from the divisive political environment and from restrictive laws. They conclude that:

[P]ublic schools increasingly are targets of conservative political groups focusing on what they term "Critical Race Theory," as well as issues of sexuality and gender identity. Schools also are impacted by political conflict tied to the growing partisan divides in our society. These political conflicts have created a broad chilling effect that has limited opportunities for students to practice respectful dialogue on controversial topics and made it harder to address rampant misinformation. The chilling effect also has led to marked declines in general support for teaching about race, racism, and racial and ethnic diversity. Principals also report sizable growth in harassment of LGBTQ+ youth. (p. viii)

In addition to these formal studies, several investigative reporters have documented examples of the laws' impact (Gluckman, 2023; Golden, 2023; Natanson, 2023). As PEN America reports:

Examined together . . . , these studies paint a comprehensive picture of the vast chilling effect that educational gag orders are having on the tens of thousands of educators—and, by extension, the millions of students—to whom they apply. Educators have accused lawmakers of trying to make it a crime to teach students about controversial topics; the record suggests that this is indeed how these laws are playing out on the ground. . . . If teachers are afraid to make any mention of race or LGBTQ+ identities in the classroom, if they are afraid to answer student questions, if quality educators are leaving and cannot be replaced, students are the ones who suffer most. (Young et al., 2023, section III)

Divisive concepts laws, book bans, and curricular interference may have a secondary impact of accentuating the divergence in curricular content, instructional methods, and school culture among states. Students in the states that have passed these laws will have a strikingly different education, particularly in areas of history, social studies, English language arts, and current social, political, and environmental issues. With limitations on programs that support health curricula and social-emotional learning, students' personal development will be differentially impacted. Even their ability to reasonably discuss controversial topics may differ sharply. The consequences of this polarization in education on future citizens can perpetuate and extend divergent worldviews that make finding consensus on factual evidence and compromise on policy issues ever more challenging.

## Saddling Up Is Worth the Risk

As educators and parents, we may shudder at the thought of entering this arena and dealing with such contentious policy issues as well as those individuals who have little regard for the hurt or fear they engender through their words and behavior. Already conflict-avoidant in general, we seek thoughtful and sincere consideration of others and respectful treatment of differences.

No one, not even those in leadership positions, feels sufficiently adept in conflict resolution skills to claim that they can routinely and productively resolve the intense conflicts that are surfacing in the politicization of education. Many feel paralyzed by the onslaught of proposals, the extent of financial support for those running for school board offices, and the misleading rhetoric of parental rights used to impose a political ideology on other parents' children.

So, the prospect of entering the arena, advocating our principles, and risking retaliation is not an experience we seek, absent a sense of urgency. Fear of the unpleasantness of these situations moves some people to turn away completely and not get involved, hoping the problem goes away. And some, recognizing and fearing the danger, remain in the shadows in the hope that others will be brave enough to take the necessary public stands.

Yet, as with those who finally confronted the carnage of McCarthyism and who advocated civil rights in the face of intense retaliation, our humanity and our values require that we act to protect our children, our schools, and our democracy. In the end, complacency and silence constitute complicity, and they support the success of those attempting to use public education for the purpose of indoctrination.

In essence, taking action is about overcoming fear. The risks are real, and we can easily become, as Lee (2006) points out, a prisoner of our own weaknesses and fears. But in acknowledging our weaknesses and fears and still "saddling up anyway," as John Wayne said, we can make a difference for today and for tomorrow.

CHAPTER 5

# Where Do We Find the Courage to Act?

*Courage is not the absence of fear but rather the assessment that something else is more important than fear.*
—FRANKLIN D. ROOSEVELT

IF THIS MOMENT IN TIME CALLS ON US TO FIND THE COURAGE TO enter the arena, take a public stand, and work to restore the positive direction that public schools have worked so hard to pursue, what steps can we take to be most effective and what sources of strength can sustain us in the process?

The first step in finding the courage to act is to understand and accept that the risks are real. If we take a stand against the banning of books, in support of equity and discussions of race and gender, and in support of enabling our children to learn the unvarnished truth about our nation's history, we can expect to be attacked by those who have gained power and who oppose these tolerant and inclusive positions. The attacks may be unpleasant and even threatening.

If we serve in policy positions such as on a school board or even as a leader of a school's PTA, we may open ourselves to being ostracized and publicly criticized by those who disagree with us. Education leaders and educators who are upstanding and outspoken may suddenly find their jobs in jeopardy, as have many superintendents, administrators, school librarians, and teachers across the country whose school boards have been taken over by individuals with extremist viewpoints.

Once we acknowledge the danger, we need to look within and appreciate that our resistance to getting involved has a rational basis. For some people, a realistic self-assessment may confirm that we find it challenging to respond effectively in situations of conflict and threat and that we feel we lack the skills to manage conflict well. Others may be torn by indecision about which action is the right one to take. Still others may fear the potential loss of friends, colleagues, and family members who disagree. For some, it is a desire to protect one's family from the threats and attacks that may result. And for others, it is a pragmatic awareness that taking a stand could result in the loss of employment, putting one's financial security at risk.

The second step is recognizing that numerous, and potentially overriding, positive consequences may result from our entering the arena. We can achieve clarity about our values and our principles and the directions we think essential to securing the well-being of our students. We can gain skills in managing difficult situations. By taking a stand, we can gain the respect of others and learn that there are many friends, colleagues, family members, and even people we do not know who appreciate the courage of our action and the voice of reason and care we project.

And if our advocacy causes us to lose our current position, there are other employers who value individuals who have taken that stance and will offer new opportunities for leadership. The bottom line: There is no greater inner satisfaction than knowing we are working to promote the values of equity, justice, care, and a fair and free education for our students and our communities.

## SOURCES OF COURAGE AND COMMITMENT

The studies of people who have entered the arena—whether they be political activists, human rights workers, or individuals who stepped forward in times of crisis—teach us that we actually have a deep well of resources within us that can support courageous action and sustain us in our efforts (Berman, 1997). A number of researchers have explored the factors that motivate and sustain social and political involvement. These studies have generally been qualitative studies that delve deeply into the life experience and background of those interviewed.

Hoehn (1983) interviewed eighty-seven adult activists, community organizers, and public officials, most of whom were middle-class citizens deeply invested in participating on behalf of the common good. Keniston (1968) studied a group of fourteen activists working on causes related to African Americans deprived of their civil rights, Vietnamese peasants deprived of their national autonomy, or the poor in the United States deprived of basic human needs. Colby and Damon (1992) explored the lives of twenty-three individuals identified as moral exemplars for their commitment to helping others. Jennings (1992) interviewed twenty-eight human-rights activists in California, thirteen of whom were volunteers and fifteen of whom were employed in human-rights organizations.

Oliner and Oliner (1988) studied 406 rescuers of Jews during the Holocaust and compared them to 126 nonrescuers who were similar in sex, age, education, and geographic location during World War II. Rosenhan (1972) conducted extensive interviews with forty-six "freedom riders" who participated in America's Civil Rights Movement. Clary and Miller (1986) replicated Rosenhan's study with 162 volunteer crisis counselors. Daloz et al.

(1996) studied one hundred individuals who had made a commitment to the "common good" that stretched across political lines.

These studies are filled with personal insights and experiences of individuals who entered and sustained their involvement in the social and political arena. Across all of the studies, the research indicates that interest in participation and actual activism are stimulated by three core motivations:

- the unity of one's sense of self and one's morality,
- the sense of connectedness to others, and
- the sense of meaning that one derives from contributing to something larger than oneself. (Berman, 1997)

Awareness of these three factors can influence our own choices.

We possess a moral compass that guides us and leads us to act in ways that enable us to ground our decisions and actions in the values and principles we hold dear. We feel a connection to others and to our environment that leads us to act in caring and responsive ways to those in need. And each of us wants to feel that we have a legacy and have made a difference . . . that we have made the world a bit better for our participation in it. Each of these factors connects to one's everyday experience, and the strength of each motivation correlates with one's level of activism.

The individuals in these studies were ordinary people who stepped forward to address those in need or respond to injustices that violated their moral values. Moral integrity played a significant role in their motivation. When we reflect on those orientations and aspirations in ourselves, we can find the strength and courage to enter the arena.

The rescuers of Jews during the Holocaust put their own and their families' lives at risk in the context of a campaign of political and ethnic terror. Oliner and Oliner (1988) found that many were motivated by the need to respond to something they found deeply unethical and immoral. As one rescuer described his motivation, "I found it incomprehensible and inadmissible that for religious reasons or as a result of religious choice, Jews would be persecuted. It's like saving somebody who is drowning. You don't ask them what God they pray to. You just go and save them" (p. 167). Another said, "I knew they were taking them and that they wouldn't come back. I didn't think I could live with knowing that I could have done something" (p. 167).

An interviewee in Hoehn's 1983 study stated, "I couldn't shake off the notion that suffering hurts and that I'm in a position to alleviate it sometimes. I have seen suffering, and just because I would prefer not to be bothered by it, that doesn't take away my responsibilities. It doesn't take away my consciousness. I can't just say, 'Well to hell with suffering, I've done my share'" (p. 25).

A long-term civil rights worker interviewed by Colby and Damon (1992) said, "I knew that the things we were working for were right. When times get bad, you only have one thing to fall back on—that you believe in what you are doing" (p. 123). Youniss and Yates (1999) summarized the research on the interaction between identity and moral action by concluding that "everyday morality seems to be rooted in an essential identity rather than being mediated by calculated reason" (p. 361).

Understanding what we value and what principles guide us enables us to follow our moral compass. Yet having a sense of moral integrity is not the only motivation. What these researchers found is that the sense of connection with others, the sense of care for others, serves as a second resource and impetus for giving people the courage to act.

Jennings (1992), who studied human-rights activists, concluded that "a response to human-rights violations and human need is practically linked to a sense of self defined through connection and affiliation with others" (p. 3). One of his interviewees who worked to promote human rights in Central America explained her motivation in helping people she didn't know by saying that "they're part of my life, they're part of my family" (p. 17).

Oliner and Oliner (1988) reported this same importance given to connection, generosity, and care:

> Already more accustomed to view social relationships in terms of generosity and care rather than reciprocity, [rescuers] are less inclined to assess costs in times of great crisis. Already more deeply and widely attached to others, they find it difficult to refrain from action. Already more inclined to include outsiders in their sphere of concern, they find no reason to exclude them in an emergency. Unable to comprehend or tolerate brutality as anything but destructive of the very fabric that gives their lives order and meaning, they react in much the same way as if caught in a flood—holding back the tide through whatever means possible. (p. 251)

In attempting to answer the question of how people become committed to the common good, Daloz et al. (1996) describe the larger scope of connection that developed over time among their interviewees:

> The people we interviewed have learned that they and all others are an integral part of the fundamental interdependence of life. Knowing this, when faced with a violation of what they know to be true, they cannot not act. Their commitment derives from knowing that we are bound to one another and to the planet; it is as untenable to turn away from the world's pain and unrealized potential as to abandon one's child or sever one's hand. (pp. 195–196)

The third major motivator of the courage to become engaged is to find meaning, make a contribution of value, and leave a positive legacy behind. The renowned psychologist Erik Erikson (1968) describes this quality as finding the intersection of one's personal history and history itself. The research studies show that the courage to act also derives from the desire for meaning that takes one beyond oneself, to feel that one is contributing to the welfare of others and society. As explained by one of the persons Daloz (1996) and his colleagues interviewed, "This is what I love, what my purpose is, what drives me, and makes me happy" (p. 197).

Colby and Damon (1992) discuss this sense of meaning and its importance to the exemplars they studied:

> We believe it is accurate to say that, among the twenty-three exemplars, there was a common sense of faith in the human potential to realize its ideals. Although the substance of the faith and its ideals was too varied and too elusive to be captured in a final generalization, it can perhaps best be described as an intimation of transcendence: a faith in something above and beyond self. The final paradox of our study is that the exemplars' unity of self was realized through their faith in a meaning greater than self. (p. 311)

Other commonalities emerged from these studies. For most of the individuals interviewed, the causes they chose were not concerned with improving their own condition but instead with alleviating injustice and harm to others. They also acted without the guarantee of success and felt fulfilled by promoting good in the world, living out their values, and experiencing connection with others.

In general, the researchers found these individuals firm in their values but not rigid or ideological. They tended to be open-minded and personally honest. Colby and Damon (1992) note that "even as the exemplars' grip on their core ideals remained unwavering, they continued to reexamine their most fundamental attitudes and choices at frequent intervals" (p. 184). They credit this to their open-mindedness and their openness to the perspectives of others and to being changed by those perspectives.

But above all else the researchers pointed out that those they interviewed were ordinary people who felt compelled to act.

Oliner and Oliner (1988) put it this way, "Rescuers are not saints but ordinary people who nonetheless were capable of overcoming their human frailties by virtue of their caring capacities" (p. 239).

The resources that enabled the individuals in these studies to have the courage to act are not exceptional but reside within each of us. We experience moral integrity in our hearts and guts. We appreciate the sense of connection and care with others and the value of extending that care to those in need. We find meaning in doing things of value for others and for the community, and we want our legacy to be that we contributed to making our society a better place.

## ENSURING THE WELL-BEING OF CHILDREN

By standing against book bans, divisive concepts laws, attacks on DEI (diversity, equity, and inclusion) initiatives, limitations on discussions of race and gender identity, elimination of programs designed to support the social and emotional development of children, and the effort to endorse specific religious beliefs within public school classrooms, we stand in support of ensuring the well-being of all our children, of affirming that schools should provide equitable access for all, and of providing students with the knowledge and skills that can sustain our democracy. When asked about the risk of taking action, one interviewee of Daloz et al. responded with a sentiment that was echoed through many of their interviews. "Risk?" the person responded. "The greater risk is in not doing it" (p. 197). As another interviewee shared, "Success is not the measure of a human being, effort is" (Daloz et al., 1996, p. 200).

Responding to the attacks on education today also entails standing against the threats and abuse that target educators, education leaders, and parents. It means standing with those who attempt to take an active role in policy leadership and in support of depoliticizing our schools and bringing respect and consideration to the way people treat each other. And it calls for meeting the challenges of this moment in history by advancing the civic mission of education to support more inclusive and democratic governance. This work is all about integrity, connection, and meaning.

So, where do we find the courage to act? We find it deep within ourselves, within the motivators that guide our daily lives, and we find it within our connection to others who share a common moral compass. We need to revisit these sources of courage regularly and intentionally, because these issues will be with us well into the future.

CHAPTER 6

# What Journey Are You On?

*Life shrinks or expands in proportion to one's courage.*
—ANAÏS NIN

PROBABLY EVERY PERSON AT ONE TIME OR ANOTHER IN THEIR
life has faced a situation that made them think—sometimes
fleetingly, sometimes in depth—about how courageous they were
willing and able to be. What was the event, time, person, or other
circumstance that made you stop and reflect on your current journey toward taking courageous stands and actions? While some
facets of a personal journey may appear to be accidental, and others incidental, with awareness we realize that most steps along the
way are intentional or self-directed, the result of our own choices
and decisions.

As we encourage you to think about your personal journey,
we feel it is only fair—and important—to share pieces of our own
journeys . . . stories that tell of our private and public struggles
to demonstrate courage in the face of difficult circumstances as
educators and community leaders.

Some journeys pave pathways to success; others derive their
worth from the effort made and the perseverance to hold fast

to the values and principles that constitute our moral compass. Taking courageous action comes with no guarantees of success— only the self-acknowledgment derived from knowing that we are continuing to make incremental progress in the development and expression of a personal moral principle that helps to define the person we are and the contribution we make to the world.

## LUVELLE BROWN: ADVANCING EQUITY

Equity is a word frequently, almost casually, sprinkled in conversations today. That is both good and bad. Good, because it means that people are thinking about the concept. Bad, because people can interpret or even misinterpret the term differently, sometimes in ways that are diametrically opposed. In general parlance, people take the word to mean fairness or impartiality, leveling up a situation based on the circumstances. However, some people confuse equity with equality, which is a misinterpretation.

Equality means treating all parties the same regardless of circumstances. For example, picture a father who is preparing dinner for his two children. One child is six years old, while the other is six months old. Giving both children a hamburger would be equal but not equitable, because there is no consideration of their different needs; strict equality would be detrimental to the infant who is better served by strained peaches.

In a nation of laws, Americans generally stand up for equality as a foundational principle of our government, especially with regard to legal status and rights—although sometimes Lady Liberty still must take her scales into court. In a court of law, the application of equity can remedy a situation that would be unfairly adjudicated if only the inflexible common laws of equality were taken into account. It often requires a combination of both equality and equity to promote comparable levels of opportunity for all participants in an activity—which is not to say that identical outcomes can be assured.

Alas, while the cause of equality has achieved notable and hard-fought gains in the centuries since the precolonial era, equity has not fared as well, and the marginalization of identifiable groups of people has continued through the generations. With the rising use of the term "equity" in social justice circles, individuals with a right-wing extremist ideology sometimes view the word as code for discrimination against whites. That is most unfortunate, as a word that should be held up as a goal of our society instead leaves people's lips as an epithet.

And therein lies the challenge that forms the basis of my life's work—to bring not just equality but equity to the students of my school district and the families of my community. The seeds were planted as I watched my parents fight for justice in the schools of my youth, and the germination continued during the formative years of my career in education. In ways small and large, I strove to promote equity throughout my classroom as a teacher and throughout my school as a principal. In 2011, as I moved to a larger stage as a school district superintendent, I took with me that commitment to equity. Unknown to me at that time, my principles were about to be tested in the crucible of school district leadership, and I would need to summon courage as I arrived at a crossroads.

My commitment to the authentic journey of providing access and opportunities for all has been tested and deeply cemented on at least two occasions. In March 2017, I was named Superintendent of the Year by the New York State Council of School Superintendents. Admittedly proud of this recognition, I invited my parents and siblings to attend the award ceremony. Before long, my name was announced, and I was invited to come to the stage and accept the award. But before I could leave my chair, my mother reached out and put her hand on my arm. Looking me squarely in the eye, she said, "They can give you all the awards they wish, but you've done nothing until you change the way this room looks."

Slightly chagrined, I looked around. The conference attendees consisted of New York superintendents and their cabinet members. The people in the room were White and mostly male. As a member of the group, I knew that statewide only 3 percent of superintendents were people of color, and only 30 percent were women. So I had not expected the group to look otherwise.

However, my mother and other immediate family members were visiting the state of New York for the first time. Hailing from Virginia, they had been told they were visiting the most diverse state in the nation. They expected the leadership of the public schools to mirror the vaunted diversity of the state. Their disappointment and dismay were plain to see.

I should have anticipated my family members' shock at the leadership's makeup. Unfortunately, over time I had become accustomed to the lack of diversity. Not only was representation from marginalized populations sorely lacking in leadership positions but the teacher ranks were disproportionate as well.

The soon-to-be-released *See Our Truth* research report from the Education Trust–New York (2017) shared alarming statistics regarding the lack of diversity among teachers in New York State Schools.

- Ten percent of Latino and Black students—more than 115,000—attended schools that had no teachers of their same race or ethnicity.

- Latino and Black students in districts outside of the five biggest school districts (New York City, Buffalo, Rochester, Yonkers, and Syracuse) were nearly thirteen times more likely than their Big 5 peers to have no exposure at all to teachers of their same race/ethnicity.

- Nearly half of the state's White students—48 percent or 560,000—were enrolled in schools without exposure to a single Latino or Black teacher.

The report revealed similar findings relative to the diversity of the state schools' administrative leaders. At the time of this book's publication, these data have seen no significant change.

As for my mother's comment, at what should have been one of the proudest moments of my life and even a bit of a crowning achievement, her words jarred me out of my complacency. They signaled the abrupt end to my current path and the beginning of a different and more authentic journey.

At that moment in the award ceremony, I decided to ditch my prepared remarks and address our state superintendent and other leadership colleagues from across the state in an unscripted manner. Accordingly, I shared that while honored to be receiving this special recognition, I now found myself inspired to do much more to provide loving access and opportunities to all students, in part by cultivating a leadership pipeline that would include many more women and people of color, thus changing the way that room looked.

I watched as some of my colleagues in the room began to appear uncomfortable, shifting in their seats and stealing glances at the rest of the audience. Perhaps some of them felt chastened for not recognizing (as I had also not seen) the homogeneity in the space. On the other hand, in the coming days, I also received a few admonishing emails stating that my acceptance speech was neither the time nor the place for such a proclamation. (Exactly what was the appropriate time and place, no one said.)

As one of the few people of color in the state and even in the nation to hold the position of superintendent, I knew that stepping out even further on this philosophical ledge to criticize the very institutions that I had been successfully navigating would spark resistance. I admit to feeling some trepidation, wondering if I were about to jeopardize my career. I now realized that the academic journey I was on could win me awards, but the more authentic and bolder path could get me fired. Yet my mother's words reverberated in my heart and mind more clearly than did the criticisms of colleagues, and I responded to the call to courage.

With the utmost intention, just as I had used my platform at the award ceremony, I began to use my newly anointed status as Superintendent of the Year to influence meaningful changes. For example, in December 2017, I worked with the state's superintendents association and another African American superintendent, L. Oliver Robinson, to create and co-chair the New York State Council of School Superintendents' Commission on Diversity and Inclusivity.

Since then, this committee of superintendents from across New York has undertaken the specific charge of identifying, supporting, and influencing policies with the purpose of increasing the number of people of color serving as school superintendents. We also posit that increasing the diversity in the highest leadership role requires a more culturally responsive approach to teacher recruitment and retention as well as more responsive classroom instructional practices.

Beginning in 2017, this commission has held statewide and regional professional development events, engaged in advocacy efforts, and been a strong proponent of statewide DEI initiatives. Still, the data have not shifted in a positive direction, largely due to the lack of consistent statewide efforts to address the fundamental issues leading to underrepresentation in leadership roles. The majority of district board members have not received training in implicit bias, and they lack the awareness to detect and remove race-based barriers.

Additionally, as detailed in the *See Our Truth* report (Education Trust, 2017), the task is made more challenging by the dwindling number of educators of color in New York. Reversing this trend is taking longer than we had hoped, but the Commission remains determined to make a difference on behalf of our students and staff, who deserve the opportunity to see the best that people of all races and backgrounds have to offer.

While continuing to work on behalf of equity on a statewide basis, I was still fully engaged as the leader of Ithaca City School District (ICSD). I realized that I could not expect to have credibility in my state-level efforts if I did not have my own house in order. Thus began the leadership journey that led to the second test of my commitment to equity.

In reflecting on our district's academic performance, I proposed to staff that it would be beneficial to conduct a critical analysis of students' enrollment in various course offerings, with a particular focus on the area of math. Essentially, I asked our instructional team, "What's happening? What is responsible for the variations in student outcomes?"

In short order, the answers came rolling in. ICSD educators saw clearly that the current instructional program included multiple tiers of academic grouping with the lowest being populated by those students perceived to have the fewest skills and the lowest levels of achievement. In the district as a whole, 22 percent of students were Black, Latino, or multiracial, but students of color made up a disproportionate share of learners in lower-level math classes.

For example, in the fall of 2017, one teacher's lowest-tier class consisted of 70 percent non-White students. These numbers were consistent across the middle schools. During a public board meeting, when staff were asked, "What's happening?" one teacher bluntly responded, "We are just perpetuating institutional racism here."

We dug deeper. Middle school teachers determined that the recommendations from teachers at the end of fifth grade, along with the selection process for class enrollment, were too subjective. Some teachers remarked that they felt pressured by parents (mostly white) to recommend their children for the more accelerated math courses. And some minority students were starting to absorb the incorrect perception that high-level math courses were beyond their understanding and grasp, so they and their parents saw no reason to push for enrollment.

While middle school teachers were grappling with the enrollment patterns, high school math teachers were expressing significant concerns regarding incoming students' preparation for high school courses. The high school teachers felt that students enrolled in accelerated classes during middle school were racing through content without developing the deep understanding and skills needed for success in more demanding courses. Meanwhile, students in the lower-tier classes had received no exposure at all to key concepts and skills, and it was highly unlikely they could now make up so much lost ground.

With the enrollment and grouping patterns appearing to harm our student outcomes rather than help them, ICSD joined multiple districts around the nation that were seeking a better approach (Berwick, 2019). At the same time, strengthening our resolve, the National Council of Supervisors of Mathematics (2016) recommended that districts eliminate tracking in middle school math.

This group of educators from throughout the nation pointed to flat or declining test scores as a call to action to change existing practices. Their findings were later confirmed by the National Center for Education Statistics (2022), which found that results on the National Assessment of Educational Progress (NAEP) had been flat for a decade with just 26 percent of students testing proficient in 2022.

The NAEP testing results, coupled with the report from the NCSM, were noteworthy. Additionally, a review of research revealed that while "high-ability" students are academically successful in any grouping style, heterogeneous grouping offers the greatest social and emotional benefits, including participation and confidence. Finally, we knew anecdotally that mathematics achievement, often measured by standardized tests, had been used locally and nationally as a gatekeeping tool to sort and rank students by race, gender, and socioeconomic class.

In the spring of 2018, after reviewing the research and also consulting with the leadership of the National Council of Teachers of Mathematics (NCTM), ICSD approved a one-school pilot program to begin in the fall that involved collapsing math for eighth graders from three tracks to two: algebra and eighth-grade math. Teachers developed strategies to offer differentiated pedagogy to students of varied proficiency levels enrolled in the same course.

In fall 2019, the pilot expanded to all eighth-grade math classes at all middle schools. Then, in fall 2020, the pilot became a scaled initiative involving all sixth- and seventh-grade math classes. At those grade levels, instead of being assigned to standard versus accelerated tracks, all students would be grouped heterogeneously. At that point, with all middle school students now to be affected by the new grouping procedures, what had been muted rumbles of parental dissatisfaction erupted in a burst of fury.

While taken aback by the vehemence of some parents' responses, I was not completely unaware of their views. For the previous two years, I had kept my ear to the ground on this issue and had tried the usual strategies to promote involvement, understanding, and acceptance. As part of the planning and communication efforts in advance of implementing the heterogeneous grouping plan, the school district's administrative leaders, in partnership with teachers, held multiple community information sessions. But as beneficial and commonsensical as this proposal seemed to those of us who had designed it, its districtwide implementation sparked significant opposition.

Immediately upon the district's move from a one-school/one-grade pilot to a consistently executed approach to grouping students for mathematics instruction, resistance arose among some parents and others. The plan was no longer affecting just some students in some grades in some schools. It was every-body—and now it was personal.

Those disagreeing with the shift were primarily families who had previously expected and been granted access to the advanced-level math courses with other students they perceived to have exceptional math skills similar to those of their own children. They cited their belief that the heterogeneous group-ing would result in a weaker academic experience for their more academic-minded and higher-achieving children.

During the information sessions, now in their third year, some parents protested the student grouping and instructional shifts, expressing their displeasure with the decision, questioning the schools' and school district's leadership, and demanding a pause or reversal of the plan. One parent created a petition that was eventually signed by hundreds of others, insisting that the administration or school board intervene and reverse the decision. Though the uproar occurred around the same time as the district's annual school board elections, the board was solidly in support of the mathematics instruction and grouping change and the imple-mentation continued.

The weeks went by. Even with our best intentions and strong support from teachers and the board for the curricular shift, the stakeholders who had enjoyed the privileges of the previous student-grouping strategies were steadfast in their criticisms and efforts to reverse the decision. I knew how uncomfortable some members of our community had become about this divisiveness, and I understood that this segment of the community was not accustomed to being uncomfortable when engaging with our schools. I also knew that taking on such a powerful group of community members could result in casualties—and I might be one of them.

The coordinated efforts to interrupt my decisions and leader-ship proved unsuccessful at this point in time; but, as I learned, those same individuals found other ways to criticize, scrutinize, and disrupt our strategic efforts in other areas. Our commitment not to prejudge students' academic capacities had brought forth detractors who were angered by our decisions and were determined to undermine any opportunities for us to make future decisions that could threaten what they considered to be their rightful privileges.

Repercussions followed. The next year, one incumbent board member who had served for twelve years lost to a parent who ran an energetic, two-week campaign. While the winner campaigned on multiple issues, she received particularly substantial support from voters opposed to heterogeneous grouping. The loss of a long-serving board member, the public criticism of my leadership, and other negative consequences were part of the pressures my district supporters and I endured as we strove to overturn once and for all an oppressive practice of student grouping.

Losing supportive board members and seeing the growing number of folks who questioned my leadership, I knew that the courageous decision to lead a student grouping effort that was grounded in research, best practice, and teacher voice might irreconcilably diminish the trust placed in me by an influential and powerful group of community members. Angering this vocal and connected segment of the community would not only manifest itself by way of challenges on the current math decisions, but would motivate this group to scrutinize future decisions, challenge my overall leadership, and mobilize other like-minded people to seek seats on the board with the goal of disrupting and potentially reversing any disliked policies and approaches, possibly culminating in my removal as superintendent.

It was time to ramp up our strategies for maintaining what we believed in—equity for every student. With the dedicated support of teachers, administrators, and even some parents who rallied to the cause, we adopted a three-pronged approach. First, we inundated our school community with education about why we were making the shift and how we planned to ensure success.

Month after month, we provided consistent, transparent, and information-rich communications by way of community meetings, websites, emails, and newsletters. There was no escaping our message.

Second, we extended support to our school-based and central office leadership as they dealt with the dissenters face-to-face in sometimes uncomfortable circumstances. The administrators who were at the forefront of this initiative chose to remain in their roles during a challenging time and continued to grow as instructional leaders. Their positional stability contributed enormously to the community's confidence in the district and its decisions.

Finally, and perhaps most persuasive and meaningful of all, we solicited student voice. After all, students would be the ultimate recipients of whatever decisions held sway. We solicited students' testimonials and held panel discussions devoted to their perspectives. Audiences heard from students who had performed very well in our previous system as well as from students who had found the former approach to mathematics grouping to be problematic. Our students were unafraid to speak truth to power. They demanded a better system and were poised to hold us accountable for the delivery of the high-quality education they needed and deserved.

Ultimately, we managed to hold off the naysayers and stay the course. We implemented an instructional initiative that was grounded in careful thinking and intended to provide equitable access and opportunities for all students, especially those who had previously been underrepresented in our highest-level math course offerings. Additionally, we sought to reverse a practice that had been perpetrated for generations in our school community, despite producing negative results for particular student populations. Thus concluded a second call to courage—a time when I had to stand up and hold firm to an expression of equity that I believed was fair to all students while righting a wrong that had been visited on some of them.

So as I look back on my journey on behalf of equity—a journey that has had many twists and turns and is far from over—again I ponder the meaning of equity. During the pandemic, as much of our professional work was being conducted virtually, I was leading professional development for school districts across the nation. Many of the districts were grappling with how to respond to the murder of George Floyd and the resulting racial reckoning in our country, as well as how to address the stagnant and declining student achievement by young people from marginalized backgrounds.

Much of the focus of my professional development workshops centered on how to engineer teaching and learning experiences that meet the needs of all learners irrespective of their identities, especially those learners who had not been performing well in traditional school settings. As I led these virtual sessions from my home office, one or both of my children (son age ten and daughter age eleven) would often be in the same room, but off-camera.

On one particular occasion, I was reviewing the definition of diversity with hundreds of educators in a virtual environment. My explanation of the term, along with some of the participants' questions and resistance to the word diversity, apparently alarmed my children who were listening.

After completing the session for the adult learners and closing my computer, I noticed the shocked and perplexed looks on my children's faces. When I asked what was troubling them, they responded that they were puzzled to hear how much conversation was needed to establish adults' common understanding of diversity. My children have been reared to see diversity in all spaces and to recognize the beauty of learning and interacting with folks of various identities. They couldn't fathom why this simple concept was apparently so complicated for adults to grasp.

Handing me a Marvel Comics book, my son pointed to an image of the X-Men to express his understanding and appreciation for diversity. (Non-spoiler alert: The X-Men represent a wide range of identities including class, gender, religious orientation, nationality, ethnicity, physical appearance, and special ability.) He suggested that I use this comic book image in future workshops as a metaphor for how young people understand and appreciate the intersections of various cultures in schools and the broader society. Remarking that the X-Men are powerful and beautiful because of their diversity, he also noted that in the stories they are marginalized and oppressed through laws and aggressions due to the fears and misunderstandings of the dominant race and culture.

These comic book stories were created during the 1960s. Isn't it past time for America's journey to equity to reach its destination?

## SHELDON BERMAN: RESISTING RESEGREGATION

Sometimes we recognize the journey we're on through thoughtful reflection, but more frequently clarity comes in moments of crisis when our values and principles are tested. The incubation of my personal beliefs and values occurred over a period of years; however, leading a district in the throes of a fight over desegregation—a fight we did not win—brought them unexpectedly and quite publicly to the forefront.

As a social studies teacher in the 1970s and 1980s, I had been proud of our nation's progress in school integration, despite protests and resistance to court-ordered mandates. In 2007, newly appointed as superintendent of Jefferson County Public Schools (JCPS) in Louisville, Kentucky, I found myself inheriting a U.S. Supreme Court decision that had just ruled unconstitutional the student assignment plan that supported integration in the school district. I did not fully realize it at the time, but my courage was about to be tested and my values would be on the line.

First, a bit of history. The glaring and nationwide disparity between schools serving Black versus White students in the 1970s produced federal, and generally court-supervised, efforts to desegregate public schools. Faced with entrenched patterns of segregated housing, school districts turned to such tools as bus-ing, redrawing of school boundaries, and magnet programs in an attempt to integrate their schools. Although early desegregation efforts were marked by protests, federal orders and court supervi-sion ensured that district leaders and school boards continued to make progress.

From the 1970s through the late 1980s, the percentage of students attending desegregated schools expanded. At the height of the nation's desegregation efforts in 1988, nearly half of African American students in the South attended integrated schools. Yet as districts achieved their desegregation goals and were declared unitary, concerted forces began to turn back the clock toward more segregated neighborhood schools. Since 1988, schools have resegregated to levels that existed in 1970 (Black, 2011). A few examples follow:

- In 1969, U.S. District Court Judge James McMillan ordered North Carolina's Charlotte-Mecklenburg Schools (CMS) to use "all known ways of desegregating, including busing." The U.S. Supreme Court upheld this decision in Swann v. Charlotte-Mecklenburg Board of Education, 402 U.S. 1 (1971), making *Swann* a landmark case and setting the precedent for school desegregation cases across the nation. Following a court challenge to the plan in 1999, CMS began a slow dissolution of its student assignment plan. By 2007, student assignment had given way to neigh-borhood schools, with some parental choice among schools.

- Seattle was one of the few cities that implemented a vol-untary busing plan in the 1970s to promote integration. By the late 1980s, the plan was modified to a controlled choice approach that allowed families to rank their preferred schools. Mandatory busing was phased out in the late 1990s and an integration-promoting race-based tiebreaker was applied when a school had more applicants than openings. However, a lawsuit was filed by Parents Involved in Community Schools and a 2007 Supreme Court decision (Parents Involved in Community Schools v. Seattle School District No. 1, 551 U.S. 701 (2007)) overturned the modest tiebreaker proposal. Seattle's 2009 student assignment plan redrew school boundaries to promote greater diversity, but also guaranteed that students could attend their neighborhood schools.

- Given the declining support for race-based plans, Wake County, North Carolina, a national leader in desegregation efforts, adopted in 2000 a socioeconomic plan requiring that no school's population exceed 40 percent free- or reduced-price-lunch students. However, the 2009 election of four school board members adamantly opposed to the student assignment plan caused not only the abandonment of the plan but extensive political disruption, including the resignation of the superintendent.

The story was a similar one in community after community across America. However, Jefferson County Public Schools (JCPS), with its nearly 100,000 students, took a different stance. In the mid-1970s, JCPS (predominantly suburban and White) and the Louisville Independent School District (predominantly inner-city and Black) faced an economic conundrum. With school operations heavily dependent upon local property taxes, the financial status of the Louisville district was becoming increasingly unstable.

The leaders of the Louisville district recognized that its students were not receiving an appropriate education. The local NAACP and the Kentucky Commission on Human Rights were reaching the same conclusion and mounted a legal fight for better education of the community's African American students. By state law, county school systems were required to absorb any financially dissolving district within its geographic boundaries. Accordingly, to the consternation of both districts, a state-forced merger was imminent.

Discussions of that prospect brought the districts' acknowledged racial disparity into dead center of all operational planning. Multiple race-related cases were filed in court. In April 1975, the consolidation of the two districts—with vastly different systems of transportation, food service, financial accounting, teacher training, salary assignment, curriculum and instruction, building maintenance, and so on—took effect. It was a massive upheaval, and many nervous parents began looking for other places to educate their children, even if it meant moving to a neighboring county. Small private schools quickly expanded and new ones were established.

In July 1975, a federal judge ordered the barely merged district to simultaneously desegregate—by September. The district complied, though not every employee and board member was supportive. School opened on schedule, but for weeks, groups of White parents took to the streets in protest. Rocks were thrown at buses carrying Black students through White neighborhoods. The National Guard was called out to ensure students' safety while being transported. As cold weather arrived, the protesters dwindled in number, but the protest signs proliferated and the anger was barely contained. White flight ensued and, within a few years, more than 40,000 students from the original two districts had left the merged district.

In the coming decades, the community became more accustomed to the desegregation process; while many citizens saw its value, busing remained highly unpopular. The judge's 1975 decree was followed by repeated court-approved adjustments in the student assignment plan to keep the countywide schools racially balanced in the midst of White flight and intra-county population shifts.

Then, in 2000, a lawsuit filed on behalf of several African American students, who wanted to attend the community's historically Black high school without regard for racial balance, prompted a federal judge to lift the desegregation order and declare the district unitary. Busing for the sake of desegregation was no longer a federal requirement.

In the interim, however, twenty-five years of school integration had exposed community leaders to the benefits of districtwide diversity for a city with an increasingly multicultural population, and the elected school board voted to continue voluntary integration through reliance on a managed choice plan that included cross-district busing of some White students and most Black students. More legal challenges ensued, this time from White suburban parents; yet Louisville's long-time mayor Jerry Abramson and the Louisville Chamber of Commerce boldly took a strong and public stand in support of the student assignment plan, agreeing with the briefs filed by social scientists who defended the value of integrated schools.

Helping to cement the integrated approach was the vote of the local citizenry to consolidate city and county governments into one metro government, effective January 2003. However, in 2007, to the dismay of many community and education leaders, the JCPS student assignment plan was overturned by the U.S. Supreme Court (*Parents Involved*). In a 4–1–4 opinion, the court struck down the use of individual-student-based racial classification for assigning students to schools, while acknowledging that districts retain a compelling interest in seeking diversity and avoiding racial isolation through both race-neutral and race-conscious means.

This watershed decision was delivered just two days before I was slated to take on the leadership of the district. During the wide-ranging and community-involved interview process for the superintendent position, it had been clear in almost every setting that the community and its leadership wanted to retain an integrated school district even if the Supreme Court eventually ruled against the district. In those interviews, questions about my commitment to integration were raised by central office administrators, editors of the *Courier-Journal* (Louisville's daily newspaper), teacher union leadership, Greater Louisville Inc. (the local Chamber of Commerce), the school board, and the general public.

In each meeting, I made clear that we would pursue every avenue and nuance left open by any court decision in an effort to preserve an integrated school district. It was also clear that the school board, business community, teacher leadership, and administration believed that an integrated system created better opportunities for youth and a better community as a whole. After being at the helm of a suburban Boston school district for fourteen years, I was excited about the opportunity to make a difference in an urban district that had already established itself as a pillar in the effort to provide an integrated environment for students.

There was a great deal of research evidence to support taking that stand in spite of the national trends in the reverse direction. The research on the benefits of integrated schools is extensive and powerful. Eaton and Chirichigno (2011) found that "racial diversity in schools does carry long-term social benefits. These include reduced neighborhood, college and workplace segregation, higher levels of social cohesion and a reduced likelihood for racial prejudice" (p. 1).

Numerous studies have found beneficial outcomes of desegregation, including that students who attend racially and socioeconomically diverse schools are more likely to achieve higher test scores and better grades, to graduate from high school, and to attend and graduate from college compared with their otherwise like counterparts who attend schools with high concentrations of low-income and/or disadvantaged minority youth (Bohrnstedt et al., 2015; Frankenberg et al., 2016; Johnson & Nazaryan, 2019; Mickelson & Nkomo, 2012; Pettigrew & Tropp, 2006; Reardon & Owens, 2014; Tegeler et al., 2011).

An advisory from the U.S. Department of Education (2011) stated, "The academic achievement of students at racially isolated schools often lags behind that of their peers at more diverse schools. Racially isolated schools often have fewer effective teachers, higher teacher turnover rates, less rigorous curricular resources (e.g., college preparatory courses), and inferior facilities and other educational resources" (p. 1).

Integrated schools matter. They may have the greatest impact on economically disadvantaged and minority students, but they improve the academic and social experience of all students. Integrated schools also matter to the future of our nation. And they resonate with the values I hold dear around ending systemic and institutional racism; supporting equity, diversity, and inclusion; and pursuing social justice.

Because of the broad commitment to desegregation, when the Supreme Court decision came down, the district was able to issue an impassioned document *No Retreat: JCPS Commitment to School Desegregation* (Jefferson County Public Schools, 2008), vowing to find another path that would continue the rich history and success of desegregation in Louisville's schools. In that document, we wrote that, "At a time when schools nationwide move away from policies to mitigate segregation, Jefferson County Public Schools are not—and will not—give up on providing schools that, as Justice Anthony Kennedy wrote, continue 'the important work of bringing together students of different racial, ethnic, and economic backgrounds'" (*Parents Involved*, 2007).

To chart a course, I convened a team of twenty individuals including attorneys, demographers, and central office administrators. Undaunted in our determination to preserve what the district and community had fought for through so many years, the district crafted a new student assignment plan based on the socioeconomics of entire neighborhoods, relying on factors that have an impact on student success in school—such as family income level and adults' level of education, in addition to minority status.

The plan won accolades from many. Daniel Kiel, in his *Fordham Law Review* discussion of JCPS's 2008 student assignment plan, found that, "rather than submitting to the fate of losing hard-gained student diversity, JCPS has adopted a novel student assignment plan that is a model for districts seeking to capture the educational benefits of diverse schools without running afoul of the U.S. Constitution" (Kiel, 2010, p. 2876).

The initial results were very positive. Not only did the vast majority of elementary parents receive their first- or second-choice school but 59 percent of the ninety elementary schools met the plan's racial integration parameters and another 34 percent were progressing toward that goal. Meanwhile, 76 percent of middle and high schools met the guidelines. In addition, the proportion of school-aged children residing in Jefferson County attending JCPS continued to climb, exceeding 80 percent.

In 2009, the district reviewed NAEP demographic data from the *Trial Urban District Assessment* (National Center for Education Statistics, 2010), as well as data from more than two dozen districts that serve urban areas and have large student populations. This analysis revealed that Louisville had the smallest proportion of highly segregated schools in the nation. Fewer than 5 percent of JCPS schools had student populations that were more than four-fifths minority or more than four-fifths White, while the comparison cities generally had more than 75 percent of their schools operating at those extremes.

The plan also broke ground in another area. In the prior busing plan, students in the predominantly Black northwest end of the county were integrated with largely poor or working-class White students in the southwest end of the county while preserving the wealthier east-end exchanges of students. The plan shifted this economic imbalance so that for the first time, west-end Black students would be able to access some of the highest-performing schools in the district. This change was of significant value to the Black families in the west end but eventually escalated parental and school board tensions over the student assignment plan in the east end.

Despite the success, another lawsuit was filed by parents trying to overturn the new student assignment plan. Notwithstanding significant decreases in student transportation times, the busing issue dominated the local media, which focused on the vocal naysayers who no longer believed diversity was worth the inconvenience of busing. The rise of the Tea Party and the highly publicized abandonment of voluntary integration by other districts placed increasing pressure on the members of the JCPS board, who faced strident opposition in their election races. A growing chorus of voices demanded a return to neighborhood schools, even though existing housing patterns would inevitably resegregate schools and reconcentrate poverty in the schools located in the city's core.

Student assignment became an issue in both the mayoral and gubernatorial elections. Although Louisville's mayor has no jurisdiction over the public schools, one candidate for mayor aired commercials indicating he would correct the "failed student assignment plan." The president of the Kentucky Senate, also a candidate for governor, sponsored a state bill to give all students a right to attend the school closest to their residence. This attempt to use a highly emotional educational issue as leverage for political advantage further inflamed the electorate, making it even more difficult for the voices of reason to promote the benefits of diverse schools and seek adjustments to the plan that would meet the needs of more families.

Buffeted from all sides, JCPS requested support from the U.S. Department of Education. The short two-page guidance statement issued by USDE in 2008 essentially affirmed Justice John Roberts's 2007 opinion that "strongly encourages the use of race-neutral methods for assigning students" (*Parents Involved*, 2007). The NAACP's Legal Defense Fund quickly attacked the guidance as inaccurate, stating "there is no requirement in *Parents*

*Involved* that school districts only use race-neutral means to promote the compelling interests in diversity and avoiding racial isolation in their schools," but the damage was done.

By 2010, the pressure on the JCPS school board members was so great that they voted to adjust the plan. Privately, a couple of board members made it clear to me that they were interested in essentially abandoning the plan and that other members of the board were similarly inclined. One state senator, who had been supportive of the numerous district improvement efforts initiated during my tenure, shared with me that, "We love what you are doing to improve education for our children but if you want to survive you will have to abandon the efforts to retain the student assignment plan." Others shared the same message. With the board member who was the strongest advocate for the plan resigning due to health concerns, I could see that the board and I were on divergent paths.

Hoping to find a compromise, I reconvened the team that had developed the initial plan and we began to devise modifications that would decrease the growing public controversy. We determined that it might be possible to reduce the number of bused students by identifying areas within a school's geographic boundaries that were in contrast to its majority demographics. Including those subareas in our analysis would enable us to increase the number of students who could remain in their neighborhood schools without compromising our efforts to maintain our diversity guideline. However, it was too late. It became clear that the board was going to pursue a different path—with or without me.

In the fall of 2010, the board voted to not renew my contract. Then, once the modified plan was proposed, the board indicated it would reconsider that vote. It was clear to me that at best I would have a divided board and that the expectation would be to abandon or even more significantly modify the plan. My commitment to retaining and sustaining an integrated district would not be possible.

For me, this was a crisis-in-courage moment. I could potentially retain a position in a community I had come to love and in a district that I enjoyed leading by compromising my values and commitment, forever knowing that I had disassembled a plan that was bringing equity and inclusivity to young people—or I could leave. On the evening when the board was reconsidering the vote on extending my contract, I informed them that I would be leaving at the end of the year and there was no need to take that vote.

My expectation that the board would move in a different direction came true shortly after my departure. The board hired as superintendent an individual who, as an interim superintendent in another state, had dismantled that district's desegregation plan after its superintendent resigned in protest of the board's decision to abandon their plan.

In December 2011, too late to influence the battle in Louisville over busing, USDE retracted its 2008 guidance statement, which had been contested by the NAACP, and issued a lengthy guidance (United States Department of Justice–Civil Rights Division & United States Department of Education–Office of Civil Rights, 2011) outlining race-neutral and race-conscious strategies. However, even then, USDE offered little monitoring or advocacy to support districts' struggles to maintain voluntary integration.

In 2012, the JCPS board chose, in effect, to abandon the intent of its 2008 plan, instead adopting a plan that, with additional changes over time, has gradually but significantly lessened most schools' level of integration and returned multiple schools to having student populations that are majority minority.

In spite of two unanimous board votes initially approving a student assignment plan that would have maintained the district's rich history of integration, the social and political pressures on the JCPS board and administration created waves that added Louisville to the long list of districts—including Seattle, Charlotte-Mecklenburg, and Wake County—that essentially capitulated to the resegregation of the district. As hard as the decision was for me, standing up for the values I held and still hold dear was the right one.

The hard-learned lesson of recent decades is that, lacking either strong community support or federal mandate, school districts and committed superintendents and school boards have not survived and cannot survive the political turmoil created by busing and other race-conscious means of desegregation. Far too many superintendents have left their positions, voluntarily or otherwise, rather than lead the dismantling of their districts' integration plans.

If our nation is to thrive, there is an urgent need to regenerate a national conversation about the growing racial and ethnic segregation in our schools. We need to engender support from key community leaders, including local government and faith-based organizations, for an approach to student assignment that fosters and sustains school diversity. These leaders should broadly frame the diversity dialogue around revitalizing the community, enhancing economic opportunity, strengthening educational opportunity, and preparing students to participate in a democracy, all of which can result from an integrated school district.

In the meantime, our efforts to support DEI programs and maintain the conversation about race and racism are critical as openers to the larger conversation about systemic and institutional racism. The vestiges of racism and de jure segregation still linger. We continue to slip back into a "separate but equal" philosophy that didn't work in the pre-1970s era and won't work now to close the achievement and opportunity gaps.

I still believe that it is our moral and civic obligation to prevent complacency from undermining the dream of equitable access to quality education and an integrated civil society. To succeed, we must revive the conversation about integration and social justice in our communities and at a national level. Courageous leadership doesn't mean doing what's easy or what's popular. It means doing what is right for children and for the future of our nation over the long term.

For the authors, the writing of this book is another step in pursuit of a more equitable, inclusive, and just society that enables the success of all children. It is a way to hand on both what we've learned about courage and what we hope we can collectively achieve by pushing back against the efforts of individuals with extremist views and by continuing to advance educational equity for all.

CHAPTER 7

# How Do We Reclaim the Narrative?

*The epidemic of "alternative facts," or what I call "compromised truth," is one of the most insidious and dangerous global systemic risks of our time. Compromised truth is the single greatest threat to humanity: It topples our ability to make ethical decisions. It undercuts trust and our distinction between right and wrong. It sets every one of the drivers of contagion of unethical behavior into motion. . . . And it undergirds every societal risk we face, from climate change to global pandemics to the demise of democracy.*
—SUSAN LIAUTAUD (2021, P. 153)

INDIVIDUALS WITH RIGHT-WING EXTREMIST VIEWS HAVE BEEN effective in getting their ideas across relative to culture war issues. Couched in language about parental rights, liberty, transparency, accountability, government overreach, and moral upbringing, the messages can be persuasive. Yet beneath the verbiage of faux patriotism, each of the issue campaigns features a different—sometimes explicit and sometimes implicit—message that is simple, yet distorted and misleading. What follows is a sampling of these extremist campaign messages:

- "Equity" is code for discrimination against White people.
- Racism is a relic of the past that's now being used to give minorities an unfair advantage.
- Wokeness is a blasphemous, left-wing attack on White people and traditional American and religious values.
- The left distorts the great history of this country, calling it unjust and blaming today's White children for those injustices. This focus on past injustices undermines patriotism and turns children against the United States.
- There is an American way and those who come to this country or want to live in this country need to accept the norms, traditions, and beliefs about being an American.
- Schools have become left-wing bastions of propaganda and are indoctrinating children into leftist ideologies, such as critical race theory.
- School library books and classroom books about identity, sexuality, and diverse family structures are grooming children to become homosexuals and transsexuals.
- Learning about diverse family structures, including LGBTQ+ families, exposes children prematurely to inappropriate sexual content.
- The goal of social-emotional learning "is to psychologically manipulate students to accept the progressive ideology that supports gender fluidity, sexual preference exploration, and systemic oppression" (Moms for Liberty, n.d., p. 3).
- Discussions of identity, sexuality, and justice are the province of parents, not schools, and schools are stealing that right from parents.
- Banning books and restricting what is taught preserves parents' rights and ensures that children retain the innocence and joy of childhood.

- Religion is the founding principle of this country and ensuring that schools promote Christian religious values enables all students to pursue moral lives.

The core message undergirding each of these statements is that children and the country as a whole are being undermined by minorities and leftists who want to destroy traditional, White Christian, American culture—the culture they claim has made America great. In much the same way as McCarthyism's message did in the 1950s, the current extremist message seeks to weaponize fear and faith in pursuit of right-wing ideological dominance.

Each of these issue statements is deeply flawed. None is supported by data or research. In essence, these statements represent a historical narrative divorced from the reality of American history and the essential diversity of races, cultures, religions, and beliefs in our society. The statements are meant to play on people's fear of losing power, authority, and status while promoting division and hate for those who are somehow "different." They paint anyone who disagrees with this perspective as unpatriotic and immoral, intent on grooming children to behave and believe in unnatural and unpatriotic ways. They particularly play on parents' fear for their children by telling them that schools are deliberately brainwashing and damaging children.

When taken together these messages are dangerous because they support division and polarization and oppose core democratic principles of respect for diversity, inclusion of difference, and dialogue and compromise for the benefit of the common good. Instead, they move people toward dogmatism and authoritarianism by seeking to impose the will of the believers on others rather than respecting diversity, honoring each person's humanity, and pursuing common solutions or compromises.

For these individuals with extremist positions, the battle isn't about finding common ground and building consensus around our differences; it's about winning by any means possible, including distortion, lies, personal attacks, threats, and violence. Some of these individuals have no illusions about the messages' false and covert political intentions; they know exactly how and why the issue campaigns have been designed to divide communities. However, many other people have fallen prey to the messages and are convinced of their veracity, despite the lack of supporting evidence, and truly fear for their children's safety and well-being.

The hydra-like multiplicity of messages, attacking many fronts at the same time, and the vehemence with which they are delivered, make them both intimidating and challenging to respond to. Still, we cannot let such messages go unchallenged. We must respond, while not engaging in the viciousness involved in the conversations or replicating the strategies that individuals with extremist views use. How can parents, educators, and education leaders respond in a meaningful and effective way while preserving integrity and decency?

## RESPONDING TO INTIMIDATION AND THREATS

First, we can't allow ourselves to be intimidated by the threats or personal attacks. To do so and to back away is exactly why these threats and personal attacks are being made. To back away is to solidify the extremist perception of us as weak. To back away is to silently condone or enable unacceptable and sometimes unconscionable behavior. It only further empowers those who think such acts will enable them to achieve their ends.

There is a relationship between right-wing rhetoric and those on the fringe who take words to the extreme of violence, whether against a California store owner who hangs a Pride flag outside her store, or against Black clerks and customers at a Dollar General in Jacksonville, Florida, or against Jews praying in a Pittsburgh synagogue. These are not disconnected events. They are the extension of the rhetoric of hate behind so many of the messages. The rhetoric of hate and vilification may seem to be mere words, but all too often those words motivate someone to commit violent acts.

Second, these pernicious and vile acts need to be confronted directly and we, as citizens of a democracy, need to hold the perpetrators and our elected officials at all levels accountable. We can call out and confront the disrespectful, vilifying, and threatening comments of individuals when they happen in personal exchanges, at meetings, and in public sessions. Even though some individuals have been convinced of the normalcy of these messages as a result of continual exposure to them via social media and televised outlets, most people understand the problematic nature of demeaning and disrespecting others.

For most individuals, calling out the unacceptability of the behavior without vilifying the person in return is key to stopping the behavior while still respecting the person. For those who continue or who escalate threats in person or via social media, we have a responsibility to call on the community and law enforcement to respond. As the Anti-Defamation League (ADL) so clearly articulates, there is no place for hate in our schools and our communities. We can neither accept nor condone nor ignore such behavior.

On the other hand, standing up and calling out this hurtful and harmful behavior has a powerful impact. It affirms for ourselves and those around us not only the importance of respect for others but the strength of the principles we stand for. It also serves to articulate a different narrative that counters the misinformation and disinformation behind these statements. And it serves as a model for other adults and for children of how to respond in challenging situations when confronted with extremism and hate.

## We Have More in Common

It's important to realize that although right-wing extremists may be highly vocal right now, they still represent only a small minority. Although they are well-organized and have been strategic in securing positions of authority at the local, state, and national levels, most Americans, even those who lean toward conservative perspectives, don't agree with their positions or the stridency of their tactics. In the long term, we need to build upon the good will and common sense of those who are not on the fringes in order to intervene and stop individuals with extremist positions by making their rhetoric and their actions patently unacceptable to the larger public.

Prior to the mid-2010s, these extreme voices existed but largely kept to themselves and were socially ostracized. Since then, political, societal, and social media forces have enabled them to not only come to the surface but to be supported by particular political leaders and social and television media outlets. The movement we need to create is one that brings us back to normalcy in the way we respect each other and the way we honor diversity within our common social fabric.

Among the broad spectrum of people, there is more agreement than disagreement. For example, the Fordham Institute—a conservative Washington, D.C., think tank—studied the perspectives of individuals who identified as Republican or Democrat regarding their views on social-emotional learning (SEL). The report's major finding was that nearly all parents, regardless of political persuasion, want their children to acquire social-emotional skills and believe that schools have a role to play in providing that instruction. In addition to overall support for social-emotional skills, the study found that parents within both political parties generally affirm the importance of a wide range of specific SEL skills such as goal setting; navigating social situations; empathizing with others; standing up for people of different backgrounds; responding ethically; and understanding, expressing, and controlling emotions. Although parents who identified as Republican were not supportive of the term "social-emotional learning," in part due to the right-wing media attacks on the term, the study concluded that "when SEL-related programs are described without jargon, support soars on both sides of the aisle" (Tyner, 2021, p. 10).

The Pew Research Center, surveying over three thousand parents of school-age children who took part in the American Trends Panel, found something very similar on the topic of social-emotional learning. The center reported that "about two-thirds of parents say it is extremely or very important to them that their children's school teaches them to develop social and emotional skills" (Horowitz, 2022, p. 8).

In fact, the study found that in spite of differences about what is taught, parents, regardless of their political party, were largely satisfied with the quality and approach of their children's school. The study reports that:

> Republican and Democratic parents of K–12 students have widely different views on what their children should learn at school about gender identity, slavery and other topics. . . . At the same time, Republican and Democratic parents—including those with children in public schools—are equally likely to say they are extremely or very satisfied with the quality of the education their children are receiving (58 percent of each party) and that the teachers and administrators at their children's schools have values that are similar to their own (54 percent each). (Horowitz, 2022, p. 4)

However, even in areas where there is disagreement, a percentage of parents from both parties share common views. For example, 24 percent of Republican parents agree with the majority of Democratic parents that "the legacy of slavery still affects the position of Black people in American society today" (Horowitz, 2022, p. 6). Republican and Democratic parents are largely in agreement about the amount of time their children's school spends on core academic subjects, with 71 percent of Republican and 75 percent of Democratic parents indicating that it is about the right amount of time.

In the area of how satisfied parents are with how much say they have in what their children learn, 77 percent of Republican parents and 82 percent of Democratic parents are either extremely, very, or somewhat satisfied, with only 22 percent of Republican parents and 16 percent of Democratic parents indicating that they are either not too or not at all satisfied (Horowitz, 2022). There is much agreement to build on that can counter the false narrative that public schools are bastions of left-wing ideology intent on converting children to their cause.

## Focusing on Core Purposes

In order to reclaim the narrative, we can bring people together around shared goals and experiences instead of dividing groups into "us" and "them." We can call people in rather than calling them out, that is, take inclusive approaches that build on and support common ground rather than personally attacking individuals for their beliefs. That doesn't mean we avoid correcting misinformation and disinformation or critiquing the tactics of those who use lies, distortions, and threats to convince others. However, we must become adept in approaches and messaging that move the public away from inflammatory rhetoric and slogans and toward an accurate focus on the core of what we want to accomplish. This core often constitutes common ground for the majority of parents and community members.

For example, as both the Thomas B. Fordham Institute and the Pew Research Center found, parents strongly support the essential skills embodied in social-emotional learning—self-awareness, self-management, social awareness, relationship skills, and responsible decision-making. The common ground we can articulate is that families want schools to create learning environments that are safe, positive, and productive for all students and that prepare students with life skills for success in school and work. When done well, social-emotional learning is the best vehicle to accomplish that goal.

Common ground in the area of equity and teaching about race and ethnicity is less universal, but still attainable. Michael Petrilli, Fordham Institute's executive director, identifies five areas of general agreement in his article "The Common Ground on Race and Education That's Hiding in Plain Sight":

- Implementing culturally affirming materials.
- Diversifying the education profession.
- Maintaining high expectations for all students.
- Teaching students to empathize with others.
- Presenting painful chapters in America's history in an honest and unflinching way (Petrilli, 2021).

For most parents and community members, the essential common ground is wanting all students—regardless of race, economic status, gender, or country of origin—to feel included and be successful. That is the essence of our equity work.

As for countering censorship, the common goal is to help young people become knowledgeable and responsible citizens in our democratic society by giving them full and accurate information, as well as multiple perspectives on historical and current events that enable them to draw informed conclusions. And as for culturally responsive teaching, all students need to see their cultures reflected in the books they read and the instruction they receive in order to feel included and respected.

These core-purpose messages are ones we can all help to deliver. As superintendent of Virginia Beach City Public Schools, Aaron Spence worked to educate the public, stake out common ground, and calm the chaotic environment engendered by an anti-CRT campaign. Among his communications efforts, he published an op-ed stating:

We know empirically that academic achievement requires an environment where students feel socially and emotionally secure and able to take the intellectual risks necessary to learn and flourish. Building that environment means having schools and classrooms and a school division where all students feel seen, known, cared about, included and supported—where the diversity of thought and culture and background that defines us all is welcome and where children and adults feel they belong. Surely, we can all agree on the importance of that. (Spence, 2021)

Focusing on the core purposes that unite people not only serves to defuse hot-button issues but helps educate people about why this work is so important in the first place. It also summons people's better angels rather than their divisiveness.

## COMMUNICATING THE COMMON GROUND

One of the most beneficial impacts of articulating core purposes is that it builds allies among board members, staff, parents, and community members. Reaching out and developing support is best achieved by sharing core messages with these groups, talking with them about the value of initiatives, and inviting them into the dialogue. We need to ensure that the strident voices of opposition don't drown out the voices of the majority of families and the interests of those who have traditionally been marginalized.

We also must be open to conversations with those who express concern about initiatives, striving to understand their fears and encouraging them to recognize the programs' positive outcomes. Many people may not fully realize that the information they have received is inaccurate and misleading. We can try to allay their fears and concerns by engaging in a civil and reasoned dialogue on the core purposes of our efforts and by building on respect for each other's humanity. At the same time, we must humbly acknowledge that the concerns being expressed may represent issues we ourselves need to address or changes we need to make to be more inclusive.

However, we may not be able to dispel all of the zero-sum thinking, conspiracy theories, and misinformation, or to accommodate the deeply held religious or political beliefs of some individuals. We may not be able to convince them that assisting traditionally marginalized students lifts all students. The current level of polarization in our society has created a strong sense of tribalism around political ideology to the degree that some people see their own identity through that ideology or through the groups associated with that ideology, creating a dogmatic adherence to the ideology and the group.

Questioning that ideology is then mistakenly perceived as an attack on the person's identity. When individuals unquestioningly believe in the absolute rightness of their own views, that entrenched dogmatism prevents them from taking another's perspective or being open to considering alternatives. In such situations, once we recognize that a conversation won't have productive outcomes and that we can't create a civil and reasoned dialogue, we need to affirm our core purposes and move forward.

At the same time, it's important to avoid being drawn into emotional debates with individuals who want to derail beneficial initiatives by distorting the district's work or maligning its staff. These individuals are a minority, and some may not even be members of the community. Responding calmly and respectfully, while focusing on why the work is key to the success of all students, is a more effective approach.

A superintendent in Eugene, Oregon, once found himself in a public meeting vociferously defending a math program adoption. The school board chair leaned over and said, "Once you start defending, you're losing." He was right. Let others debate the issues; our best strategy is to stay focused on communicating the core goals, the potential common ground, and the evidence.

## SAYING WHAT NEEDS TO BE SAID

This approach demands courage and fortitude. As parents, educators, and education leaders, we may be required to voice deeply held values and demonstrate leadership within divisive and contentious environments. In such circumstances, it's not our role to say what is most popular but rather to say what needs to be said—to lead by putting forward the core purposes of the work and helping people move toward understanding and concurrence. Putting forward that message may also require reflection, practice, and rehearsal so that core concepts can be articulated even in challenging situations.

To do that under the pressure of a tense atmosphere, we need a ready grasp of the data supporting programs' efficacy. For example, research demonstrates that social-emotional learning is a proven strategy for enhancing positive youth development, academic performance, mental wellness, and positive relationships between teachers and students. Whatever the topic, we need to use existing data with intentionality to demonstrate that the effectiveness of such program initiatives as SEL, equity, culturally responsive teaching, gender identity policies, and diversity and inclusion are backed up by substantial research.

To reclaim the narrative about schools' core purposes, we must be clear about our values and our perspective—clear with ourselves and with the public. Such candor may place us at odds with decision-makers who have a different perspective. Sometimes it's more important to stand up for our values—even if it presents risks in the reactions we receive. For educators and education leaders who are employees of a board, if the board's direction is antithetical to the values we hold dear, resigning a position may demonstrate greater integrity and yield more productive consequences—both personally and professionally.

The most difficult decisions call on us to have the courage to make clear, ethical judgments and take a public stand. By articulating core outcomes for students' education, pursuing common ground among community members, and offering positive direction, we can take a stand and reclaim the narrative on the value and purpose of such important initiatives as equity, the social-emotional well-being of students, gender identity, and diversity and inclusion.

As parents, educators, and education leaders, we can enter the fray and serve as community educators. We can accept the responsibility to stand up for what is best for students, even in challenging times. Today, when students and communities need us most, we have the ability to summon the courage to speak up for consequential initiatives—and to reclaim the narrative around the full democratic purpose of schools.

CHAPTER 8

# What Does Courageous Action Look Like?

*I swore never to be silent whenever and wherever human beings endure suffering and humiliation. We must always take sides. Neutrality helps the oppressor, never the victim. Silence encourages the tormentor, never the tormented.*
—ELIE WIESEL (1986, P. 118)

RECLAIMING THE NARRATIVE AND STANDING UP FOR WHAT IS best for students requires courage. Even in the course of everyday life, committed people encounter multiple occasions and venues in which a demonstration of courageous action can make a difference.

For parents and community members, meaningful steps might include sharing personal perspectives through an op-ed submitted to a local news outlet, speaking at a school board meeting, hosting a living room dialogue for interested parents or educators, organizing campaign efforts for school board candidates, or joining and supporting organizations that are engaged in countering extremism.

For education leaders, courageous actions could include making a statement at a public or civic meeting, organizing with other leaders to craft and deliver a collective statement, speaking at a legislative hearing, or moving forward with programs that support the well-being of students and the democratic mission of education.

There are many instances of individuals in all walks of life—from students to concerned parents and from dedicated educators to community and organizational leaders—who have taken courageous action, not only in response to the words and deeds of individuals with extremist views but to get out in front of discriminatory behavior and to proactively demonstrate the values of an inclusive democracy. Knowing that any action is likely to be met with pushback, criticism, and even threats and retaliation, individuals who take courageous action demonstrate the vitality of their values and the strength of their commitment. Following are a few real-life examples of what courageous action looks like in the world of education today.

## LOUISIANA LIBRARIAN TAKES A STAND

Amanda Jones is the school librarian at Live Oak Middle School, a lifelong resident of Livingston Parish, Louisiana, the parent of a child attending the parish's schools, and the 2021 School Library Journal National Librarian of the Year. In 2022, she noticed that an upcoming meeting of the parish's Public Library Board of Control included an agenda item proposing the removal of specific books or the placement of those books in a separate section of the public library.

Fearing that this proposal could result in book bans and the censorship of titles dealing with race, sexual orientation, and gender identity, Jones decided to express her concerns. At the Board's July meeting, she read aloud the following statement as a rationale for maintaining the current policies and collection:

The citizens of our parish consist of tax payers who are white, Black, brown, gay, straight, Christian, non-Christian—people from all backgrounds and walks of life, and no one portion of the community should dictate what the rest of the citizens have access to. Just because you don't want to read it or see it, it doesn't give you the right to deny others or demand its relocation. (Jones, 2022)

Despite the noninflammatory nature of her message, she soon found herself pilloried by a Facebook group called Citizens for a New Louisiana, which accused her of wanting to retain sexually erotic and pornographic materials in the children's section. These denunciations were followed by attacks from another group calling itself Bayou State of Mind, which accused her of supporting anal sex for eleven-year-olds. Soon she was receiving online condemnations from individuals not only in her own parish but from all over the country, including a death threat from someone in Texas (Jones, 2022).

Though deeply affected by these falsehoods and threats, Amanda Jones—in her role as President of the Louisiana Association of School Librarians—continued her anti-censorship advocacy. She also founded the Livingston Parish Library Alliance and cofounded Louisiana Citizens Against Censorship to help organize with others to prevent the political censorship of Louisiana's libraries. In addition, she took on the leaders of the two groups that initially had attacked her by filing a defamation lawsuit focusing on the disinformation about her and her statements. When the judge hearing the case dismissed the suit, Jones filed an appeal of that decision. She said, "What determines winning to me is that I spoke up on behalf of myself, who was getting bullied online. I spoke out for all the LGBTQ and Black and Brown kids in my community" (Sterbenz, 2023, para. 45).

Jones' advocacy has restrained the censorship and removal of library books. Acknowledging her leadership, in 2023 the

American Association of School Librarians presented her with its prestigious Intellectual Freedom Award. Amanda Jones is a parent and an exceptional school librarian. She is also a stand-up individual who cares deeply about the rights of others and who decided to act courageously despite the threats and demeaning falsehoods that her advocacy engendered. Her willingness to confront the risks and tackle the challenges has inspired and rallied others to join in her ongoing efforts. She is only one person—but she chooses courage, and she is making a difference for many.

## MOMS LEAD EFFORT TO RECALL EXTREMIST SCHOOL BOARD MEMBERS

In 2022 in Temecula, California, three individuals espousing extremist positions were elected to the district's five-member school board. At its first public meeting following the election, the board voted 3–2 to ban the teaching of what they alleged was critical race theory in the district's schools. This action was followed by another 3–2 vote against adoption of a state-approved elementary social studies curriculum because an optional lesson included a short biography of Harvey Milk. The late Harvey Milk had been a leader in the gay rights movement and in 1978 was elected to the San Francisco Board of Supervisors. Shortly after rejecting the social studies curriculum, the Temecula board fired the district's popular superintendent.

The response by community and staff to each of these decisions by the board's new majority included significant protests and chaotic board meetings. The vote on the curriculum caused the Governor and the State Superintendent of Public Instruction to weigh in and move to override the board. High school students walked out of school in opposition to the board's decisions. And the teachers' union and other local groups filed a lawsuit protesting the board's vote on critical race theory. After realizing that their decision on the social studies curriculum violated state law, the board partially relented but still insisted on an alternative to the lesson on Harvey Milk.

The board's decisions and its aloofness to community feedback led some parents to consider the possibility of organizing a recall. Before long, an activist mother named Monica La Combe had organized a group of other Black mothers to launch the recall effort. In an interview with *The Nation*, she said, "We're going to use what's available to us—the right we have as citizens to recall. . . . I'm not a Democrat, I'm not a Republican. . . . I'm a Black mom. [I'm going to make] sure that Black voices and marginalized voices are heard and our issues are addressed" (Cavallaro, 2023, para. 8).

The recall effort has been joined by the League of United Latin American Citizens, the NAACP, the Temecula Valley teachers' union, and a local political action committee called One Temecula Valley PAC. Together, they have been able to collect more than the required number of signatures to place the recall of one of the three new school board members, the current board president, on a March 5, 2024, ballot. Regardless of the final outcome, taking a stand and getting involved reflects the admirable courage of these individuals to take decisive action to address the excesses of the current board majority and to prevent further actions that could curtail the quality of education and the rights of individuals in Temecula.

A similar situation arose in Orange Unified School District in Orange County, California. Darshan Smaaladen, the mother of a current student in the district and of two district graduates, took on the role of cochair and chief organizer of a group seeking a recall. The group's goal was to gather a sufficient number of signatures to force the recall of two school board members with extremist views. Following the election of those two members in November 2022, the board's first action was to fire the district's popular superintendent, with one day's notice while the superintendent was traveling during the winter holiday break. The board also pursued other right-wing policies, including the adoption of a gender notification policy. Led by Smaaladen, more than 18,000 signatures were gathered by three hundred volunteers who attended community gatherings, stood outside schools, and went door to door. A vote on the recall is slated for March 2024.

In addition to these recall initiatives, parents around the country took leading roles in the November 2023 school board elections. They put their time, energy, and privacy on the line to defeat candidates who had taken extremist positions in Loudoun County, Virginia; Central Bucks County, Pennsylvania; Spotsylvania County, Virginia; Linn-Mar Community School District outside Cedar Rapids, Iowa; and many other districts whose school board meetings had become the focus of taunts, threats, and manufactured chaos as a result of the controversial and often discriminatory maneuvers of board candidates and their allies who pursued extremist action. As *Newsweek* reported:

> A year ago, [Moms for Liberty] celebrated a wave of school board victories, but in Tuesday's elections, the majority of the more than 130 candidates the group endorsed in school board elections across the country lost. Every single candidate endorsed by Moms for Liberty in Minnesota, Kansas, North Carolina and Washington lost their race. The group backed 14 candidates in Iowa, but only one was successful. Similarly in Virginia, just one of the six candidates endorsed by the group won her race. The group supported 25 candidates across Ohio and five won. Nineteen candidates were endorsed for school boards in New Jersey, but only four won. (Rahman, 2023, paras. 4–7)

These losses by candidates backed by Moms for Liberty are directly attributable to parents and teachers being determined to eliminate divisiveness and politicization in board elections and to maintain their schools as safe, caring, and welcoming places.

Whether collecting signatures for candidates or working on their campaigns or even running for school board seats themselves, educators and parents are demonstrating the courage and commitment to get involved and take a stand in the best interest of students' right to an unbiased education.

## COMMUNITY MEMBERS EDUCATE OTHERS

In 2019, JJ Briscoe graduated from Gardner Edgerton High School in Gardner, Kansas, a suburban community thirty miles outside Kansas City. In 2023, though attending college in another state, he was so concerned about the actions of the Gardner Edgerton school board that he submitted an op-ed to the *Kansas Reflector* protesting the actions of the board. Just days after a student walkout at his former high school to protest board policies, Briscoe wrote:

> Our schools help create the future for our students, and watching the Gardner-Edgerton [*sic*] School District be governed by members who adhere to a divisive and derogatory agenda is disheartening, to say the least. In the aftermath of the COVID-19 pandemic, a slate of extreme ideological candidates were elected to the school board, and their dysfunction quickly pushed multiple board members to resign. Instead of holding an open and transparent process to appoint replacements, they appointed two more members who lacked qualifications but match their agenda.
>
> Since then, the board has pushed policies that have marginalized trans students, removed books from classroom shelves, opened the door to anti-government extremist groups, stifled public participation in policy discussions, and broken their own policies. Their actions have pushed key staff members out of the district, including the long-tenured high school librarian and the sponsor of the Gay-Straight Alliance club. . . . Despite unprecedented engagement from the community,

with students generating statewide and national coverage, board members refuse to change course. . . .

Too often, voters' lack of familiarity with local elections leaves community governing bodies like school boards susceptible to takeovers from ideologues. We also know this is happening in races across Kansas. Everyone needs to know who is on the ballot and hear why they are even running in the first place.

Students who will be most affected by school board members' decisions are watching. (Briscoe, 2023)

JJ Briscoe took the courageous action of offering his perspective to the entire community as a way to offer additional insight from a graduate who appreciated the education he had received. It requires courage to stand up and share a viewpoint publicly. And it is an effective way to inform and educate others.

Similarly, Pam Shernuk, a retiree and lifelong Kansan who served on the Johnson County Commission on Aging for seven years, submitted an op-ed to the *Kansas Reflector* prior to the November 2023 school board elections. She warned the community about extremist groups running candidates for board seats and encouraged all members of the community, but particularly senior citizens, to get involved. She wrote:

This year, more than ever, school board races will shape the future of our schools and the education of children. A group that calls itself "Moms for Liberty" has started a chapter in Johnson County and is running candidates for our school board races. The Southern Poverty Law Center has designated Moms for Liberty as an extremist group for its support of advocating for book bans and endorsing candidates who align with their values.

According to SPLC, "they use multiple social media platforms to target teachers and school officials, advocate for the abolition of the Department of Education, advance a conspiracy propaganda and spread hateful imagery and rhetoric against the LBGTQ community." Both the Blue Valley School District and the Olathe School District have active Moms for Liberty candidates running this fall. There may be others.

All communities deserve school boards that will champion our teachers and students, and that will be fiscally responsible for taxpayer money. . . . Stay involved and pay attention. You owe it to the generations that follow. (Shernuk, 2023, paras. 7–11, 13)

Writing and signing one's name to an op-ed in a local newspaper opens one up to criticism and attack from those who hold extremist positions. Yet it also demonstrates commitment and courage to stand up for one's principles. It opens the dialogue about these principles and helps community members think about the complexity of these issues and the consequences of their actions and votes.

## LEADERSHIP MATTERS

Those in organizational and institutional leadership positions can demonstrate the same courage to stand up and act on principles, thereby serving as exemplars for what principled leadership looks like. Revealing examples of such leadership emerged in both Virginia and Arkansas in response to new state guidelines for school policies. In Virginia, the new guidelines related to transgender youth and emanated from the Virginia Department of Education. In Arkansas, the new state guidelines directed that Arkansas high schools could no longer count credit from an Advanced Placement African American Studies class toward a student's graduation requirements. In both states, the new policies were met with local resistance.

In March 2020, the Virginia Assembly passed a law detailing protections for LGBTQ+ students. The law didn't just spell out protections for students but required districts to issue policies reflecting evidence-based best practices. The Virginia Department of Education, then under Governor Ralph Northam's leadership, issued model policy guidelines for districts to follow.

After Glenn Youngkin was elected governor in January 2022, the department reinterpreted the law and revised the policy guidelines, allowing teachers and students to misgender transgender students by requiring the use of the name and pronouns associated with each person's sex at birth. The new policy guidelines prohibit students from competing on sports teams that don't align with their sex at birth. Parents must also be notified of discussions with a student about their gender identity and if a transgender student will be using a bathroom that does not align with their sex at birth (Virginia Department of Education, 2023).

A number of school boards and superintendents have defied the Department of Education's direction to adopt policies similar to the models the state is recommending. The school districts in Arlington, Alexandria, Fairfax County, and Prince William County, as well as others, had adopted policies consistent with the earlier guidance and maintained that the new guidance discriminated against individuals based on sex. Francisco Durán, superintendent of the Arlington Public Schools, issued a statement on the district's website saying, "I oppose any policy that infringes upon the rights of our students and threatens the safety and well-being of our LGBTQIA+ students" (Zalaznick, 2023, para. 4).

The school board in Prince William County Public Schools (PWCS) issued a statement that its current nondiscrimination policy provided the appropriate supports, in compliance with state and federal laws, for transgender youth. They wrote that "PWCS already has a regulation in place to address the rights of transgender and gender-nonconforming students in our schools" and that this regulation "is consistent with both federal and state anti-discrimination laws, and PWCS employees will continue to follow this regulation" (Prince William County Public Schools, 2023, para. 5).

Alexandria City Public Schools (ACPS) Superintendent Melanie Kay-Wyatt and School Board Chair Michelle Rief issued a joint statement that "we want to reaffirm our commitment to all students, staff and families, including our LGBTQIA+ community, that ACPS will continue to both implement and develop gender affirming policies for all ACPS students" (Cullum, 2023, para. 3; Elordi, 2023, para. 12).

Although Governor Youngkin and Virginia Attorney General Jason Miyares have insisted that districts are obligated to adopt the new policy, PWCS, ACPS, and other districts have not altered their positions (Hawkins, 2023). It is likely that their resistance will be tested in court, but that prospect has not moved these districts' leadership to change their stance. The districts' defiance of what they view as discriminatory policies toward transgender youth serves as a beacon of enlightenment for others in how to take a courageous stand, despite the political forces aligned against them.

In a similar act of resistance, six high schools in Arkansas indicated that they would continue to offer the Advanced Placement African American Studies course in spite of the state's declaring that the class would not count toward students' graduation requirements, nor would the state subsidize the cost of the AP test for the course. The course was originally banned in Florida, prompting other states to consider whether to follow Florida's lead.

Arkansas' decision to refuse to allow credit toward graduation was based on two factors: (1) the state's divisive concepts law passed in 2021 that prohibits the teaching of critical race theory, and (2) a 2023 executive order issued by Governor Sarah Huckabee Sanders on her first day in office banning indoctrination and critical race theory in schools. Arkansas Education Secretary Jacob Oliva contends that the state has not had the time or resources to review the African American Studies course materials to determine whether or not they comply with the law (Associated Press, 2023; Shah, 2023).

In spite of the state's position, six high schools—including Little Rock's Central High School, which was the site of the 1957 racial desegregation crisis—indicated that they would offer the course for elective credit due to its importance for students' understanding of U.S. and state history. Jeremy Owoh, superintendent of the Jacksonville North Pulaski School District, issued a statement that "district leaders believe that the AP African American Studies course will be a valuable addition to the district's curriculum and will help our young people understand and appreciate the rich diversity of our society" (Shah, 2023, para. 3). Little Rock Central High School issued a statement that "AP African American Studies will allow students to explore the complexities, contributions, and narratives that have shaped the African American experience throughout history, including Central High School's integral connection." The district also indicated it would cover the cost of the AP exams for students (Shah, 2023, para. 8).

It is unclear whether the stands that these districts have taken in Virginia and Arkansas will prevail. Nevertheless, their determination to articulate principled reasons for their resistance and to stand up for policies and practices they believe best support the education of their students is an exemplary act of courage in the face of extremist positions affecting what students are allowed to learn.

## PREVAILING AND SUCCEEDING UNDER FIRE

Where individuals with extremist views have taken control of school boards, they have tended to almost immediately fire or force the resignations of superintendents who were popular with their communities for their progressive approaches to education. Superintendents' stands on diversity, equity, and inclusion and on LGBTQ+ issues have been lightning rods for attacks on their principles and their employment. However, in several cases, superintendents have managed to not only prevail but to successfully change the dialogue by having the courage to stand behind their principles and articulate the value these principles offer to students and families in their districts. Such has been the case for Scott Menzel in Scottsdale, Arizona, who was attacked for his support of diversity, equity, and inclusion, and for Julie Vitale in Oceanside, California, for her support of the LGBTQ+ community.

Dr. Scott Menzel began his superintendency of Scottsdale Unified School District (SUSD), a district of 22,000 students, in July 2020, after serving as a highly successful superintendent for eighteen years in three Michigan school districts. In early February 2023, Fox News Digital began a series of reports focused on an interview Menzel had done in 2019 when he was superintendent of the Washtenaw Intermediate School District in Michigan. The interview focused on Washtenaw ISD's adoption of a mission statement focused on equity, inclusion, and social justice. In one portion of a lengthy interview, Menzel discussed Robin DiAngelo's book *White Fragility*. Drawing from that portion, Fox News Digital portrayed Menzel as holding racist views against White people, stating:

> Menzel said in an interview unearthed by Fox News Digital that White people should feel "really, really uncomfortable" as he discussed "equity, inclusion and social justice." During the 2019 interview he added that the White race was "problematic."
>
> "There's a misperception that educational equity is really only for ethnically and racially diverse districts. But White people have racial identity as well, and in fact problematic racial identity that we typically avoid," he said. . . .
>
> The superintendent also said the system needed to be "dismantle[d]" to create a system of racial equity and that "privilege" needed to be called out. . . .

He went on to endorse a book by Robin DiAngelo called *White Fragility*, seen by critics as a diatribe against White people for being beneficiaries of and complicit in a "racist system." (Grossman, 2023, paras. 5–6, 11, 13)

The Fox News Digital report generated a significant response from its viewers. Someone sent a robocall to parents encouraging them to contact governing board members and call for Menzel's firing. A state senator and two state representatives wrote an open letter to the SUSD governing board calling for Menzel's immediate removal, writing that "the racist words and sentiments Menzel publicly expressed have no place in Scottsdale schools. Superintendent Menzel was hired and trusted to foster a culture of mutual respect among students, parents, and teachers. However, his racist words prove that he is incapable of doing that job" (Grossman, 2023, para. 4). In an interview with a local news station, Tom Horne, the Arizona Superintendent of Public Instruction, added his call for Menzel's resignation or dismissal.

Menzel responded that the statements drawn from the interview were taken out of context, but he also maintained the appropriateness of the statements he made in the interview. In one interview with a local television station he said,

> Regarding the statement by the three legislators, if they read the full interview they would know I didn't say anything hateful about any group. I also did not say white people are problematic. In considering the history of this country, including slavery, forced relocation and genocide of the indigenous population, Jim Crow laws, redlining, these are examples of "problematic" white racial identity. I believe that we have to look at history in order to build a better future. (Dana, 2023, para. 18)

He continued by drawing an analogy to gender discrimination.

I see my responsibility as calling out the ways the system advantages people who look like me, and disadvantages people who don't look like me. I also have two daughters, and I know that in this society being born male is an advantage over being born female. Because I had that advantage in this country, I have an additional burden and obligation to dismantle. I have an obligation to open doors for people who otherwise wouldn't have doors open. (Dana, 2023, para. 27)

Ever since joining SUSD, Menzel has been viewed as effective in promoting excellence in instruction and administration, and he is popular with parents and the community. At a February 21, 2023, board meeting, many came forward to support and defend him. As people were lining up outside prior to the meeting, a local news reporter again interviewed him. And again, he spoke to his principles and the value they hold for the students in the district.

There have been attempts across the country to demonize words like "diversity," "equity," and "inclusion." But diversity for us represents our learning community. We have diverse students from all walks of life and backgrounds, and we embrace and celebrate diversity. We also celebrate diversity of ideas. In this country, having differences of opinion is a good thing and by sitting down at the table and having civil discourse we can actually come up with better strategies to move forward.

From an equitable lens, what we're talking about it is not equal outcomes for kids. We're talking about meeting the needs of students where they are. And some students come to us with a whole host of assets, and some don't. And so as a school system, we're providing the support that each student needs rather than giving everybody the same thing when they may not need the same thing.

And then we're creating inclusive learning environments where every student feels a sense of belonging. They are welcome here no matter what their background is, no matter who

> they are, no matter what they believe, because they are part of
> our Scottsdale family. (Dana, 2023, Video interview, 02:30)

Even though the Scottsdale school board is divided politically,
the members remain supportive of Menzel and have refused to
go along with the calls to remove him. Menzel was able to frame
the core purposes of his work on diversity, equity, and inclusion
in such a way that they spoke to the common aspirations people
hold for children, independent of political perspective. He had
the courage to maintain his principles in spite of the attacks and
articulate them in ways that helped defuse the antagonism. In recognition of his clarity and ability to speak to and act on the core
purposes of the work in diversity, equity, and inclusion, Save Our
Schools Arizona acknowledged him with its Champion of Public
Education Superintendent of the Year award.

Menzel's interactions with Arizona Superintendent of Public
Instruction Tom Horne proved significant as well. Horne had
called for Menzel's removal without having ever met or talked
with him. At a town hall meeting in one of the district's high
schools, Menzel was questioned about his relationship with
Horne. Menzel replied that although the two had never spoken
in person, he would be pleased to meet with him, adding that he
hoped for Horne's success since it was critical for the education
and well-being of Arizona's children. The Scottsdale board vice
president, who knew Horne, then set up a meeting between the
two men. The 75-minute conversation was so constructive that
Horne invited Menzel to serve on his superintendent advisory
council. Later describing their meeting, Menzel said:

> We discussed a number of the statements from my interview
> related to Washtenaw ISD and I had an opportunity to help
> him understand the full context of those statements. It was an
> open and honest conversation about diversity, equity, inclusion,
> history, and the importance of our work in public education to
> ensure each child, regardless of circumstance of birth, has an

opportunity to succeed. That final point seemed to be the point where we found common ground. By the time we finished the conversation, he indicated he thought I was a reasonable person and that he was going to invite me to serve on his superintendent advisory council. (S. Menzel, personal communication, November 18, 2023)

Although the two education leaders may still disagree on various issues of policy and practice, Menzel shared that "my takeaway is that regardless of perceived differences of opinion, there is no substitute for having direct, authentic, and thoughtful conversations. We can learn so much from each other and often find ways to work in concert for the good of the children we serve" (S. Menzel, personal communication, November 18, 2023).

Julie Vitale is superintendent of Oceanside Unified School District (OUSD) in Oceanside, California, a very diverse district of 15,600 students, 60 percent of whom are of Hispanic origin. Hired as OUSD superintendent in 2018, she brought a wealth of education and administrative experience as a teacher, high school principal, curriculum and instruction coordinator, and assistant superintendent, as well as five years as superintendent in the Romoland School District in California.

Throughout her tenure as OUSD superintendent, she has provided leadership for the district to be more inclusive, providing equitable access and opportunities for all individuals. Through her leadership, the school district created a Diversity, Equity, and Inclusion (DEI) Department; passed a gender identity policy that commits the district to equitable access for all persons independent of sexual orientation, gender identity, or gender expression; issued a board proclamation supporting June as Pride month; raised the Pride flag at district offices; provided unconscious bias training for all staff; partnered with the North County LGBTQ Resource Center for staff training on inclusion; and both led the creation of and served as conference chair for the "Lead with Pride Summit," sponsored by the Association of California School Administrators (ACSA).

For these efforts and others, Oceanside USD and one other district were rated highest among California school districts by Equality California for "having extensive policies and programs to create LGBTQ inclusion for students." At the recognition ceremony, Vitale shared that "I'm a proud, gay superintendent of the Oceanside Unified School District, and I'm able to say that because of this board of education and this community who believes that everyone belongs and everyone deserves to be loved" (Nelson, 2022, para. 18).

As an openly gay individual, Vitale has not found her path to be an easy one. Both she and the district's initiatives to promote inclusion and equity have been attacked publicly and repeatedly. In June 2022, because of her leadership in the area of inclusion, Vitale was asked to offer a keynote address at Pride by the Beach, a gathering and street festival sponsored by the North County LGBTQ Resource Center. The publicity around the event resulted in numerous speakers condemning her at school board meetings.

One woman speaking at the June 14 board meeting confronted Vitale, saying, "I saw that our superintendent made the news in our beautiful Oceanside for being keynote speaker at Gay Pride on the Beach. So, that is something that you are promoting heavily in our community and here in our schools. Heterosexuals don't get a Pride month. We don't go parading our sexuality and shoving [it] down kindergartners and first graders in our lessons. . . . Your sexuality is your choice as an adult but leave our students out of it. I mean, what is next? Bestiality? Incest?" (OUSD, 2022, June, 2:44:00).

Another speaker pulled out a Bible and issued this threat, "This is the prophecy for you, Vitale, 'Whoever causes one of these little ones who believe in me to sin, it would be better for him or her if a millstone were hung around their neck and they were to be drowned in the depths of the ocean.' You need to remember that" (OUSD, 2022, June, 3:29:00).

In a highly contentious meeting around the appropriateness of books, one individual reproached Vitale, saying, "You use your power and your position to glorify your sexuality. . . . You are bad for our city. Resign" (OUSD, 2023, February, 1:39:00).

Louis Uridel, a local gym owner who was arrested for keeping his gym open during the early months of the pandemic, called the board "groomers" for supporting inclusive LGBTQ+ policies, adding, "This woke ideology of inclusion has opened up the floodgates to the absurd, and this absurdity threatens my kids and their future." He continued by saying, "You use your relationship and position of trust with the students to exploit them in this radical gender ideology" (OUSD, 2023, February, 4:04:10). The Awaken Church called on members to speak against purportedly "pornographic" books that focused on inclusion of sexual orientation and gender identity (Nelson, 2023). And Gays Against Groomers accused Vitale and the school board of grooming students, saying, "Kidnapping, child exploitation and sex trafficking could be the result of Oceanside Unified promotion of our alphabet community" (OUSD, 2023, February, 4:08:42).

In February 2023, Wenyuan Wu, a board member of Parents Defending Education, wrote in the *California Globe* news website that "on top of the catastrophic learning outcomes, parents are horrified to find dozens of hate-filled, divisive and pornographic books in various school libraries" (Wu, 2023, para. 4). She concluded her editorial by writing that "OUSD is a microcosm of the American public education system, in which the political establishment and unionized interests have systematically hijacked one school district after another with critical race theory intersected with transgenderism. Schools are at the forefront of the cultural war waged by the far left to brainwash, radicalize, divide and sexualize impressionable kids" (Wu, 2023, para. 15).

Numerous speakers attempted to appeal to the majority of the five-member school board who were registered Republican on issues that ranged from critical race theory to lack of patriotism within the administration to pornographic books in the library. Two speakers later ran for the school board to counter the district's initiatives.

However, Vitale managed to maintain the board's and community's support for inclusivity and equity. Speakers supporting Vitale and the district's direction also came forward during the public comment section of the board agenda. They provided personal statements that spoke to the value of the district's support for inclusion, thanking the board and the superintendent for the work the district was pursuing. The individuals who ran against the district's direction ultimately lost in the election, and Vitale's contract was renewed by a unanimous vote of the board.

She reflected on her success in sustaining that commitment, writing that "I along with the Board of Education decided six years ago that we would create schools that are inclusive and affirming of all students and we called out support for our LGBTQ+ students because they are the most 'invisible.'" As a result, students, members of the GSA clubs, staff members who are gay, same-gender parents, and parents of LGBTQ+ students reported that they felt safe and supported. She writes that, "for me, this is not about courage, it is about survival and ensuring ALL of our students experience positive, affirming, safe, and inclusive schooling in OUSD" (J. Vitale, personal communication, November 21, 2023).

Being personally modest, Menzel and Vitale may not frame their efforts as courageous, but it takes courage for a leader to stand up for principles of inclusivity, equity, and diversity and the programs that sustain those principles. With the critical support of parents, teachers, and board members, both Menzel and Vitale have been successful in defending their leadership practices and positions.

Unfortunately for many other district leaders, their best efforts did not prevail against the strident and uncompromising views of extremists. In such circumstances, the responsibility devolves to the community to rally support for the election of new board members who will address the divisiveness and return the district to its educational mission. Given the influence that school board members have upon the direction of a district and the education of a community's children, such votes are among the most important any citizen can cast.

## STUDENT VOICE IN THE DIALOGUE

Year after year and decade after decade, our stunned nation has witnessed the passionate and profound courage of students in the aftermath of gun violence in America's schools. Students from Florida's Marjory Stoneman Douglas High School, Colorado's Columbine High School, and many other schools where students have lost their lives to mass shootings continue to campaign for gun law reform. Memories of the assault-weapon-based carnage that ravaged the elementary schools of Newtown, Connecticut, and Uvalde, Texas, and more schools than anyone wants to recall, fueled the anger and resolve of thousands of students who participated in an April 2023 national school walkout, demanding legislative action against gun violence.

And guns are not the only worrisome issue on students' minds. Students impacted by extremist positions in schools have also staged rallies, organized walkouts, and made presentations to school boards over changes to gender and identity policies. In 2022 in Johnson County, Kansas, a newly elected conservative school board was considering policies related to transgender students' use of bathrooms and participation in sports. With strong opinions presented at board meetings, the board decided to survey parents but not students on the issue, resulting in a student walkout at Gardner Edgerton High School. Senior Elizabeth Fiedler, the organizer of the protest, talked to a reporter from the *Kansas*

*City Star*, proclaiming, "I was outraged. Students are aware. We have made our voices known before and we will do it again. The school board is supposed to benefit students. How can they do that if they cannot even offer them the basic respect of listening to them?" (Ritter, 2022, para 3).

Students in a number of Virginia districts, including Roanoke County and Virginia Beach City, also spoke out to their school boards about transgender and LGBTQ+ policies. In 2023, sustained crowds had been present at Roanoke County school board meetings as members considered prohibiting the flying of the Pride flag and other Pride-themed symbols, adopting bathroom and sports policies for transgender children, and accepting Virginia's new model policy related to transgender children. In August, Roanoke's board became the first in Virginia to adopt the new model state policy, imposing new restrictions on transgender and gender-nonconforming youth.

Attending many of these meetings was Keely Meadows, a fifteen-year-old who passionately advocated for LGBTQ+ students. Sometimes the only student speaker, she continued to make the case to school board members for supporting LGBTQ+ students. However, that was not the only courageous leadership action she took. She organized rallies and a demonstration before one of the board meetings, attracting more than sixty students and adults. She campaigned for a write-in candidate for school board as well as two progressive candidates. Despite the lack of response from the school board and the lack of success by progressive board candidates, Meadows remains committed to attending more Roanoke school board meetings and is even helping to organize a 2024 national rally in Washington, D.C. (Rowan, 2023).

By the end of June 2023, Emily LaBar, Jay Cruz, and a group of Virginia Beach City students had been speaking at school board meetings for more than a year. Cruz and LaBar, both 2023 graduating seniors at First Colonial High School, were successful in organizing students to advocate for board passage of a policy of nondiscrimination against LGBTQ+ individuals and against approval of a proposal to create lists of library books that contained objectionable content. The nondiscrimination policy passed by the narrowest of margins (6–5) at two o'clock in the morning, coming eight hours into the meeting and after more than fifty students and numerous adults had addressed the board. It took a great deal of courage, persistence, and organizing over an extended period of time to reach that point.

In an interview with podcaster Aaryan Balu of *Pod Virginia*, LaBar and Cruz explained how they organized to achieve this outcome. LaBar stated:

> Most of our advocacy was through public comment for the past eight months; as time went on, we met with different school board members to try to develop a common understanding. In preparation for this last meeting [June 12, 2023], I talked to a lot of coalition groups, like the ACLU and the LGBT Life Center, to try to find anyone and everyone who would be able to help us. I also organized a rally outside of the school board meeting before the June 12th meeting, which was a little crazy, because I've never done anything like that before. I'd never participated in a rally before. So, I didn't know what it was supposed to look like. But I tried my best, and I think it was really successful. . . .
>
> Well, typically, there are only two weeks between each meeting. So the first week after a meeting is like a recovery. And then the second week is getting ready for the next one. So we try to get everybody's speeches done as much in advance as possible. So we can read them and help them and time them. And then, as soon as the Google Form to Speak comes out, which is maybe three or four days in advance, I fill it out first because I'm the opener. And then, I have to go individually down the list of 25 to 50 people to ensure that they fill it out and nothing technical happens. So they'll be able to speak. And then there's an issue of getting rides because a lot of the people are 14, 15, 16, they don't have a license. And if they do

have a license, sometimes they don't have a car. And we have people coming all the way from Pungo or Blackwater up to the Ocean Front. So ensuring people have a way to get there is also a challenge. (Balu, 2023, paras. 10, 17)

Cruz added, "It takes persistence. We did this for like seven months without much success. But eventually . . . Jessica Owens, a great, great school board member kind of came to bat for us and wrote a resolution" (Balu, 2023, para. 19). The meeting followed an incident at a Virginia Beach City high school where students tore down a Happy Pride Month banner. AJ Quartararo, a student from that high school, attended the June 12 board meeting and spoke of the impact that action had had and the need for the policy, saying, "Those students didn't just tear down a banner, they tore down a symbol of love and inclusivity. They tore down a feeling of security for LGBTQ+ students. I am scared for myself and I am scared for my friend and I'm scared for our future. Our community is in need of support" (Moss & LaRoue, 2023, para. 13).

These actions, according to Cruz and LaBar, achieved much more than the change in one policy. They believe that it empowered others to stand up and stand alongside them and believe that they can make a difference, not just on this issue but in their lives. As LaBar explains:

I think young people, especially young people in the queer community, can sometimes have a defeatist attitude. Because it seems like everything is going wrong, it's raining, and the sun is never going to come out. But I think our activism and the fact that we were effective, and we succeeded, is a really good sign to them that one day, it will get better. And even before this resolution passed, just that prospect for months has been getting tons and tons of kids to come and speak because they believe they can make a difference. (Balu, 2023, para. 25)

For LaBar and Cruz and for many of the other students across the country who organized rallies and walkouts, spoke at school board meetings, and met with local and state policymakers, action has been personally empowering. As Cruz shared at the end of his *Pod Virginia* interview,

> [M]y parents, sometimes they'll talk to me and be like, they'll question why am I so devoted to this? . . . I basically told them . . . I could do this every day for the rest of my life. Like, it fills me up so much. . . . [T]his isn't a one-time thing that we've taught people, [it's] a method for going about and trying to seek change, and that they can continue to keep the torch going in Virginia Beach. (Balu, 2023, para. 32)

## WE DON'T NEED TO DO IT ALONE

Acts of courage are often collective actions of a group working together to make a difference. Although a courageous act requires one person or a small group of people to get it off the ground, the collaboration and sense of common purpose among the group strengthen and enhance each individual's efforts. The support and camaraderie of individuals in Temecula and Orange Unified were responsible for getting the recall on the ballot. The combined efforts of student groups in Virginia Beach City and Roanoke County enabled these young activists to sustain their efforts over an extended period of time. Similarly, the school board election victories over candidates with extremist views are a credit to the original actions of several committed people within each community who organized action networks to inform and activate community members to get involved.

The 2023 school board election for the Pennridge School District in Bucks County, Pennsylvania, is a prime example of a small group of individuals building a large network of concerned citizens to change the direction of a district. The Pennridge School District is thirty miles north of Philadelphia and enrolls approximately 7,000 students from eight municipalities. Politically, it is a predominantly Republican region with 18,000 registered Republicans and 12,000 registered Democrats.

In 2021, a school board election had swept in a majority of board members with extremist views endorsed by Moms for Liberty. The board president for this extremist board was Joan Cullen, who attended the "Stop the Steal" rally on January 6, 2021. When the extremist board members took control in 2021, they quickly began taking actions that eventually not only frightened community members but created the motivation to elect individuals who could right the course of the district. One of the first actions of the extremist board was to eliminate the diversity, equity, and inclusion policies and disband the DEI committee. Next, claiming that critical race theory was rampant in the district and that many books contained pornography, they began a censorship campaign by removing Pride flags and specific books that dealt with race, sexual orientation, and gender.

Darren Laustsen, a local parent, became concerned that the books that were being removed from the libraries and classrooms were the same ones on the Moms for Liberty list. District policies required a formal review of any book challenge. He found that some of the books had been challenged but had passed the library's review process. Instead of following the established process, the board sought to circumvent it and make the targeted books inaccessible by marking them as checked out for the year or disposing of them through the library's "weeding" process. Laustsen filed information requests for the list of books withdrawn and weeded under Pennsylvania's Right-to-Know law, but he received only evasive responses. He finally filed a lawsuit against the district (Laustsen, 2023).

Judge Jordan Yeager, who heard the case, ordered the district not only to provide the records but to pay Laustsen's attorney's fees, writing that "the district altered the records that were the subject of the request, thwarted public access to public information, and effectuated a cover-up of . . . [the] removal of books from Pennridge High School's library shelves" (Hanna, 2023, final para.). The list of books that Laustsen eventually received matched quite closely the books on the Moms for Liberty list. As part of his efforts, Laustsen kept the community informed through social media, raising significant concern on the part of community members.

However, library books weren't the only issue in which the board attempted to evade public notice and public discussion of its actions. In addition to the book censorship, they approved a contract, posted only forty-eight hours before the board meeting at which it was to be approved, for a revision of the social studies curriculum. The contract would be with a new company entitled Vermilion, founded in March 2023 by right-wing extremist Jordan Adams. The contract would hire Adams and Vermilion to essentially replace the district's current social studies program with a program prepared by Adams, based on the far-right Hillsdale College 1776 curriculum.

Adams was a graduate of Hillsdale College and had continuing ties to his alma mater. With no experience in developing curriculum and only five years as a classroom teacher, he had launched an education consulting company to promote the adoption of curriculum in schools. Adams had spoken at the Moms for Liberty summit in Philadelphia during the summer of 2023, saying, "We should be moving on multiple policy areas and it should be happening quickly and efficiently" so that communities "cannot keep up with all of it" (Marcotte, 2023, October, para. 15). The Pennridge board's efforts to rush through a contract with Adams without teacher or public input provoked a significant negative response, with people reading sections of Vermilion's curriculum at board meetings arguing that the curriculum "whitewashed" the teaching of slavery and Native American history (Marcotte, 2023, October).

Amanda Marcotte, a reporter for *Salon* who had been covering the public concern in Pennridge, wrote that:

> The parents of Pennridge were not fooled by attempts to characterize literary fiction as "pornography." Local residents also feared that rewriting history classes to adhere to right-wing mythologies would ultimately harm the school's reputation, which could hurt both their property values and the ability of their kids to get into good colleges. Above all, multiple parents expressed a belief that schools should be preparing kids for the real world. They worried that right-wing whitewashing of history, social studies and other courses would leave kids without the basic skills necessary to thrive in a diverse, dynamic society. (Marcotte, 2023, November, para. 12)

In addition to Laustsen, a number of other parents had become concerned about the actions of the board. Pennridge parents and community members Lauren Bradley, Laura Foster, Adrienne King, and Robin Reid launched and led the RIDGE Network, formed as a nonpartisan group of engaged students, alumni, parents, and community members in the Pennridge School District, to attempt to counter the influence of the board members with extremist views. The RIDGE Network's goals are "to defend ALL students' right to a safe and welcoming learning environment, guard against threats to fair and balanced curricula and encourage respectful community engagement" (RIDGE Network, n.d., para. 1). Its website states, "We embrace a strategy of empowering the community from the ground up, facilitating leadership and student volunteer opportunities, data driven decision making and advocating for changes with a real impact" (RIDGE Network, n.d., para. 1).

Bolstered by social media posts from Jane Cramer, a leading community advocate, the Network's Facebook group grew to 1,400 members, with many others in the community aligned with its goals. The Network attracted members of both parties who expressed concern about the board's impact on the quality of education, the reputation of their community, and the spread of propaganda to children through ideologically oriented and misleading information (Marcotte, 2023, October).

The organizing, networking, and campaigning undertaken by RIDGE Network members resulted in Democrats being elected to all five of the open board seats in the 2023 election and becoming the majority on the board. Amanda Marcotte concluded her reporting on the election by writing that, "the [extremist] group was meant to put a family-friendly gloss on right-wing extremism. Instead, they got parents and teachers, many who barely have time to work and care for their families, to become political organizers" (Marcotte, 2023, November, para. 14).

A small group of committed community members have set in motion a significant change in the direction of the Pennridge School District. Like Lauren Bradley, Laura Foster, Adrienne King, Robin Reid, Jane Cramer, and Darren Laustsen, many individuals in other communities have come forward to provide leadership for organizing efforts and for founding local, state, and national organizations to combat extremism.

As noted earlier in this chapter, Monica La Combe helped launch the recall efforts in Temecula, and Darshan Smaaladen organized people to gather sufficient signatures to recall board members in Orange Unified. Amanda Jones founded Livingston Parish Library Alliance and cofounded Louisiana Citizens Against Censorship to respond to censorship efforts in her Parish and across the state of Louisiana.

Further examples include Elizabeth Mikitarian, a retired kindergarten teacher who founded Stop Moms for Liberty. Ohio mother Katie Paris founded Red, Wine and Blue, a national organization supporting women to take action against extremism in education. And Amanda Litman, a New York mother, cofounded Run for Something to encourage progressive individuals to run for office against individuals who took extremist positions.

But people don't have to found organizations to get involved. A first courageous act can simply be to join with others who are actively involved in countering extremism in public schools and the politicization of education. Numerous organizations, such as Save Our Schools, have local and state chapters that are rallying to this effort. The key to success is simple: Step forward and get involved. Make your voice and your time count.

## LESSONS IN COURAGEOUS ACTION

As illustrated by the events relayed in this chapter, taking courageous action does not require exceptional talents or even exceptional people. Every one of us is capable of courage if we are willing to step forward, speak out, and act on our beliefs. It also isn't necessary to go it alone, although speaking out for the first time may feel like venturing beyond the false curtain of security and safety that comes from remaining quiet. Avenues for courageous action range from speaking out to supporting groups that advocate change to running for office or campaigning for someone who is running for office. Courage is within each person's grasp, and acting with courage can make an extraordinary difference not only in the situation the person is confronting but also in inspiring others to act with courage.

While the stories of courage in this chapter are interesting to read, if all people do is read them and move on, then the stories' real purpose has failed. Their purpose is to motivate and encourage people to follow through and to emulate the individuals in these stories by speaking at board meetings, supporting board candidate campaigns, and otherwise demonstrating the courage of their convictions.

Courage such as that modeled in this chapter does require two things. First, you must be grounded in your principles and knowledgeable about your positions on an issue. Individuals who have taken extremist positions will challenge you—sometimes falsely quoting or exaggerating your statements and views.

You must have practiced speaking with conviction to be able to respond with calm assertion when faced with extremist narratives.

Second, you must recognize that the issue will not be resolved in one encounter. It is likely you will be explaining your values and stance again and again over a period of weeks or months. And meetings may not be enough—you may need to consider alliances, education forums, policy changes, and other efforts to ensure full support is devoted to each and every student.

It is also important to realize that even the successes of the individuals and groups highlighted in these pages are not permanent and could be challenged or reversed if efforts are not sustained. Although five Democrats were elected and flipped the Pennridge board, four other members remain on the board, including three who are directly affiliated with Moms for Liberty. A single new member could flip the board again.

In Virginia Beach city, in the fall of 2023, the board revised its gender-related policies to largely align with the new governor's more exclusionary model. The Gardner Edgerton district in Kansas is still essentially controlled by board members with extremist views. And while superintendents Menzel and Vitale prevailed, others have been summarily fired. There are strategies to make it more difficult to reverse the courageous actions we take. Embedding these values and ideals in policy, providing professional learning at a systemic level, and engaging in the political process to change laws at a state or national level can help prevent the chaos that arises when a group of individuals with extremist positions usurps control of local leadership.

Organizations are fluid, democracy is vulnerable, and the work is far from done. The continuation of America's nearly 250-year experiment in democracy is not guaranteed; we must approach it not only as a right but as a responsibility—one in which public education has a vital role to play in the development of the nation's citizenry.

Having courage is not a one-and-done event; it means ongoing and active resistance. It means remaining in the struggle over time and making a long-term commitment that may very well change one's life. Hopefully, the spirit of that change is the one that student Jay Cruz expressed with eloquent simplicity when he said, "It fills me up so much."

# How Do We Change the Culture from Divisive to Respectfully Collaborative?

*The definition of power as domination and control is lim-
ited; it is incomplete. There is another dimension, or form, or
experience of power that is distinctly different from pervasive
conceptions. The ignored dimension is characterized by collaboration, sharing, and mutuality. We can call this alternative
concept power with to distinguish it from power over.*
— SETH KREISBERG (1992, P. 61)

*Where the heart's deep gladness and the world's deep hunger
meet, commitment is conceived.*
— L. A. P. DALOZ ET AL. (1996, P. 198)

WE FACE A LONG-TERM CHALLENGE IN PUBLIC EDUCATION AND
as a nation—moving from the current culture of divisiveness to
one of respectful and collaborative problem-solving and moving
from actions that exert "power over" others to processes that
support "power with" others (Kreisberg, 1992). The first step in

that process, as detailed in chapter 7, is having conversations that focus on core purposes, bring clarity to issues of concern, and build common ground. Clearly, the second step, as shared in the stories of courageous action in chapter 8, is having the courage to stand up and speak out in support of important principles such as equity, diversity, inclusion, and civil and human rights. Yet the work of moving away from a culture of divisiveness involves much more than these two steps.

## THERE IS NO PLACE FOR HATE

Hate groups and the hateful and harmful conduct of individuals with extremist views have always existed. However, the divisiveness of our current culture, fomented by the political forces that prey on that divisiveness to promote their own pursuit of power, have accentuated the fear and hatred of others who have different skin color, national origin, or beliefs. The divisiveness in education has been manufactured by political interests as part of a broader attempt to recruit a demographic of voters—particularly suburban mothers—to their cause by stoking their fears with misinformation and distortions of what is taking place in schools across the country. As a result, hatred and fear—as represented in acts of violence, threats to individuals who embody difference, demeaning comments and disparaging labels about others who are seen as enemies, censorship and book bans, promotion of policies that exclude and diminish others, and segregation into self-affirming groups—have become ever more present. Accentuated through social media and purposeful disinformation, the infectiousness of hate and fear creates its own pandemic of polarization and antagonism.

Although we must strive to address the root causes of what moves people to hate and abuse those who seem different, in the immediate circumstances we are morally obligated to create safe spaces that disempower hatred in our schools and public spaces. In the same vein as the Anti-Defamation League's "No Place for

Hate" campaign, we need to publicly call out hateful and harmful actions when they happen and hold individuals accountable for those actions. As a community and a society, we have to make it clear that hateful and harmful behaviors are not acceptable ways for people to interact. We need to launch and collectively support campaigns that confront hate in order to make such behaviors socially unacceptable. Most important, civil and respectful behavior in word and deed needs to be a criterion upon which we set expectations for and judge candidates for all offices. Ignoring such disparaging behaviors, particularly on the part of individuals who hold elected office, endorses them through our silent complicity. Worse, it signals to young people that such behavior is acceptable.

In fact, when we call out this behavior, we need to make it clear that adults have the responsibility to model appropriate behavior for young people. When someone exhibits such behavior, we cannot only call it out but take the opportunity to explain why it is so problematic. We can make the point that we can disagree without attacking or humiliating those with whom we disagree, and that attacking others only accentuates the divisiveness without solving the problem people are trying to address. Degrading conduct sucks the oxygen out of a room and leaves everyone gasping for the fresh air of freedom. There is no place for demeaning, harmful, or hateful behavior in our schools and other public spaces.

But how do we go about acting in ways that enable people to constructively communicate about difference, reflect in open-minded ways about their own and others' positions on an issue, and collaboratively problem-solve to find acceptable accommodations and common-ground solutions? We already know from the research reported earlier in this book that most parents and most members of the public support the essential goals of programs that contribute to the well-being and success of all students and that the loudest voices of opposition are those of an active minority. To move forward in a meaningful way, we need not only to better educate parents and the community about the positive impact of the work that schools have been pursuing; we need to create a climate in public meetings that defuses the vehemence and dispels the rhetoric behind the attacks.

In part, the answer lies in the way we structure meetings and problem-solving sessions and in the attitude and approach we bring to those situations. Divisive behavior comes from a win-lose, us-them, either-or framework. If you win, I lose. In order for me to win, you have to lose. There is no middle ground. A win-lose framework coupled with an attitude that I have to do anything I can in order to win moves people to see attacks on individuals, threats, and even violence as fair game in order to prevail. Therefore, one step is to find ways to set agreed-upon norms and guidelines for appropriate ways to interact at meetings.

Another is to reflect on our own behavior as leaders, facilitators, and participants in these conversations so that we are modeling reflective, inclusive, and problem-solving approaches. When we call out behavior that is harmful or disrespectful to others, we have to focus on the behavior rather than demeaning the person. This is not as easy as it sounds, and it takes careful discipline in what we say and how we say it. We have to be able to call people in who have different perspectives or who have been misled about the impact of educational practices, as well as call out hateful, harmful, and polarizing behavior. To find real solutions, to the extent possible, we should strive to be hard on the problem and soft on people.

## SETTING NORMS FOR PRODUCTIVE CONVERSATION

Many professional and community groups begin meetings by setting norms for how people will treat each other and interact together. In fact, this is a strategy that teachers often use at the beginning of the year to enable students to reflect on the kind of classroom that will best support their learning. It then becomes a reference point when problems emerge and a way to talk about how to restore norms if they are ignored or violated.

Setting norms is best done through discussion among the group or community members about the guidelines that the group should attempt to honor in order to enable all group members to best work together. There are numerous examples of group norms, and they can be simple statements if people understand their meaning. For example, a concise statement of norms could be:

- Treat one another with dignity and respect.
- Listen actively.
- Be open-minded.
- Celebrate the accomplishments of others.
- Be conscious of the time you devote to talking versus listening.
- Be on time.
- Don't complain without offering a solution.

However, sometimes it's important to elaborate on what each norm looks like in action. For example, the superintendent's advisory council in the Andover Public Schools in Massachusetts developed the norms depicted in table 9.1 to guide how the group might work together to solve problems and make decisions.

Whether the situation is a working group or a public school board meeting, the norms can be posted and reiterated at the beginning of the session. Although at public meetings of governmental bodies, such as school boards, it is legally difficult to limit what a person is able to say, having norms posted and articulated can remind people that the community values productive conversation of difference and discourages accusations, name calling, threats, and remarks that are hurtful to others. The visible presence of norms sets an environment in which constructive dialogue can

## Table 9.1 Example of group-generated norms

**Group Norms and Agreements**

*Value multiple perspectives*
This includes: Bring a willingness to engage in difficult conversations; be open-minded; use active listening; ask clarifying questions; be empathetic; suspend judgment; be respectful of different opinions; agree to disagree; focus on common interests; build agendas collaboratively.

*Assume positive intent*
This includes: Assume people are participating with goodwill and aiming to be constructive; don't judge people; embrace diversity in thinking.

*Have courage and take risks*
This includes: Speak honestly; share new ideas; be transparent; speak up if someone says something hurtful; don't assume silence is agreement.

*Be purposeful*
This includes: Create focused agendas; be on time and stick to time; be fully present; no texting or emailing; express your passion and commitment for change and growth.

*Be responsible for the success of the group*
This includes: Share what you need to do your best work; take care of the needs of the group; take time to get to know each other; use humor and keep it light; put ideas on the table; express support for one another and for decisions; aim for shared understanding and consensus decisions; take advantage of and sustain positive energy; be responsive to the needs of colleagues.

*SOURCE*: ANDOVER PUBLIC SCHOOLS (2015), UNPUBLISHED MANUSCRIPT FROM WORKING GROUP.

occur and hateful or harmful behavior can be called out. This will not eliminate all polarizing or destructive behavior since some people have difficulty moving beyond a win-lose, us-them framework. However, it sets clear expectations for conversation among school board members and for public input by concerned citizens. And sometimes, it encourages an audience to monitor its own members or keep speakers in check.

## From Debate to Dialogue

As mentioned earlier, shifting from divisiveness to respectful and collaborative problem-solving requires that we be, in effect, hard on the problem and soft on people. One strategy for doing that is to move away from debates and instead create problem-solving dialogues around issues of difference. Essential to such a dialogue is the framing of the problem in a way that encompasses the perspectives of those in conflict.

For example, schools have standards for the selection of acceptable and age-appropriate instructional materials. Most school districts also have processes for reviewing challenges to those materials. If someone voices a concern, we need to shift the focus from summarily banning a specific book to examining how this book stacks up against the standards and how the standards guide curricular choices. Framing the dialogue this way invites the challenger to understand how and why decisions about instructional materials are made.

Based on prior experience and as solidified through television and social media, people tend to think of conversations about social or political ideas, or any issue where there is significant difference of opinion, as a debate or an argument, since that is typically the nature of public political discourse. In such conversations, we perceive individuals as seeking to win the argument or debate rather than pursuing common-ground solutions. We are far less comfortable with dialogue, which expects us to give serious consideration to other perspectives and to reflect on our own perspective. Dialogue is about finding solutions and coming to common understandings and as such stands in stark contrast to debate. Table 9.2 presents the elements of each approach.

In a dialogue, people listen to each other to find points of agreement rather than points of difference. Then they build on these areas of agreement to suggest solutions that may be mutually beneficial. Sometimes these areas of agreement are narrow, and the solutions resolve only a small part of the difference.

**Table 9.2 Elements of dialogue vs. debate**

| A Comparison of Dialogue and Debate | |
| --- | --- |
| Dialogue is collaborative, two or more sides working together toward common understanding. | Debate is oppositional, two sides opposing each other and attempting to prove each other wrong. |
| In dialogue, finding common ground is the goal. | In debate, winning is the goal. |
| In dialogue, one listens to the other side(s) in order to understand, find meaning, and find agreement. | In debate, one listens to the other side in order to find flaws and to counter its arguments. |
| Dialogue enlarges and possibly changes a participant's point of view. | Debate affirms a participant's own point of view. |
| Dialogue reveals assumptions for reevaluation. | Debate defends assumptions as truth. |
| Dialogue causes introspection of one's own position. | Debate causes critique of the other position. |
| Dialogue opens the possibility of reaching a better solution than any of the original solutions. | Debate defends one's own position as the best solution and excludes other solutions. |
| Dialogue creates an open-minded attitude, an openness to being wrong, and an openness to change. | Debate creates a closed-minded attitude, a determination to be right. |
| In dialogue, one submits one's best thinking, knowing that other people's reflections will help improve rather than undermine it. | In debate, one submits one's best thinking and defends it against challenges to show that it is right. |
| Dialogue calls for temporarily suspending one's beliefs. | Debate calls for investing wholeheartedly in one's beliefs. |

| | |
|---|---|
| In dialogue, one searches for basic agreements. | In debate, one searches for glaring differences. |
| In dialogue, one finds strengths in the other positions. | In debate, one searches for flaws and weaknesses in the other positions. |
| Dialogue involves real concern for the other person and seeks to not alienate or offend the other person. | Debate involves countering the other positions without focusing on feelings or relationships and often belittles or depreciates the other person for their beliefs. |
| Dialogue assumes that many people have pieces of the answer and that together they can put them into a workable solution. | Debate assumes that there is a right answer and that someone has it. |
| Dialogue remains open-ended. | Debate implies a conclusion. |

*SOURCE:* BERMAN (1985).

However, they have value in that they serve as a starting point for building relationships that can grow over time as individuals feel they are being heard and their viewpoints respected.

In community forums and focus groups that include representatives of different perspectives, it is possible to structure conversations as dialogues rather than debates. If all participants understand that differences exist and they commit to deeper understanding of others' perspectives, self-reflection on their own perspective, and pursuit of common-ground solutions, it's possible to shift away from divisiveness toward common understanding. This doesn't necessarily mean that all people will agree or that the group will find the ultimate solution to differences on issues but that the group may find viable paths to respect differences and move forward without demeaning each other. And in situations where decisions are made by majority rule, dialogue enables an equal consciousness of finding a balance that protects the rights of the minority.

The process of dialogue is distinctly different. Examples of questions that help facilitate dialogue include:

- What did you hear that you can agree with?
- What is at the heart of your concern?
- What might be a solution that addresses the concerns that have been expressed?

Facilitators can also prompt people to listen for certain things by suggesting:

- As you listen, you may hear things you disagree with. Try to listen also for things you can agree with and we'll discuss them afterward.
- As we begin the discussion, I want to acknowledge that uncomfortable emotions may come up. We are all here

because we care so deeply—we love our children and want what's best for them. Try to be aware of your emotions as they arise and know that it's okay to feel uncomfortable sometimes; it's all part of learning to work together to find common solutions.

Facilitating or even participating in dialogue can be personally challenging because it opens us up to the possibility of change in our own perspective. Normally, we tend to be drawn toward the confirmation of our own perspective (as is commonly reflected in our choice of everything from news broadcasts and magazines to artwork and menu selections), but dialogue requires us to thoughtfully examine our own beliefs and consider another's perspective. Doing so can create some cognitive and psychological discomfort, as evidenced by the reflexive tendency to become anxious or agitated. Having an awareness that we may be required to tolerate discomfort and ambiguity as we seek common ground is an important part of the process. We are called on to model ways of being with others that aren't divisive. This doesn't mean that we give up our principles and values or positions on particular issues. It does mean that we are able to articulate them in clear and respectful ways and also listen to others to hear their concerns as an expression of their principles and values.

## LEADING COURAGEOUSLY THROUGH DIALOGUE

Applying strategies of dialogue instead of debate is an effective way to dial back the temperature on a heated discussion. Still, it is easier said than done. Dialogue skills should be intentionally developed and practiced in nonconfrontational settings, as in a staff meeting or around the family dinner table, before the need arises to apply them in the midst of a challenging encounter.

But what if we find ourselves about to lead a discussion among participants who have no known facility in dialogue? In such a case, before the group tackles a potentially contentious issue, the leader may want to discuss a few group norms and then present the group with an opportunity to practice respectful listening and other skills by sharing their views on a lighter topic. Taking five minutes to hone behavioral expectations over a matter of no consequence may pay dividends when the discussion turns to more divisive issues.

To change the nature of our conversations and move away from divisiveness, courageous leaders need to develop mastery in facilitating and navigating difficult conversations. The ultimate goal for the inevitable discussions about sociopolitical, educational, and other complex issues should be multiparty dialogues in which everyone learns something from the other participant(s). However, such a constructive conversation requires a strategic and thoughtful approach that includes the leader's understanding of the feelings, identities, and perspectives each person brings with them. Therefore, the courageous leader—whether a school superintendent, teacher, parent, or board member—must commit to the focused listening and questioning that are needed to gain clarity and understanding.

First, the leader must seek to understand what took place in the past or what is happening currently to spark the conversation and interaction. Too often, people get into a nonproductive cycle of trying to figure out which story is "right" and which story is "wrong," when instead they should devote their energy to understanding one another. This exploration of one another's experiences and how they have contributed to the current situation is more productive than attacking—and it gives each person an opportunity to feel heard.

Courageous leaders also begin by identifying the feelings and emotions connected to the situation and conversation. This step is important because emotions can quickly overpower any of the exploration and learning that must happen. The emotions tend to be consequential because some element of the situation or conversation is threatening an aspect of one's identity. Most people, particularly those who have been traditionally marginalized, experience significant emotional reactions when they perceive an erasure of their history and culture, when they don't see themselves represented in curricular materials, when the pedagogy isn't accounting for their different cultural behaviors and learning styles, and when they are feeling unheard and unseen.

When emotions prompted by threats to one's identity appear in the midst of conversations, differing perspectives are sure to emerge—sometimes explosively. While it is challenging to facilitate such a conversation, courageous leaders need to welcome multiple perspectives in all dialogues. Diversity of perspectives drives innovation, irrespective of the industry. For example, in the K–12 education sector, the passion, energy, and commitment that are present in school board and other public meetings can serve as a model for the level of engagement needed to improve systems that have marginalized groups of citizens—whether on the basis of race, nationality, disability, gender, or another criterion.

Recognizing the high level of engagement that is required for significant change, courageous leaders would be wise to harness that constructive energy for the development of systems and policies that will meet the needs of all learners. Our nation's history documents the ways some citizens have been excluded from public education offerings or have received inequitable treatment at the hands of those in power—sometimes for generations. As keen observers of the social scene, these marginalized individuals know that recognition and collective effort on their behalf can result in education policies that cultivate a sense of belonging as well as systems intended to meet their unique needs—whether that means up-to-date instructional resources for minority-majority schools or bathroom choices for trans students. Consequently, these individuals—students as well as their parents—repeatedly appear at public meetings to advocate for their inclusion and equitable treatment. Though their public comments and requests have met with uneven levels of acceptance and action, the struggle continues and they are determined their quest will not be denied.

Meanwhile, the extent of engagement and advocacy by inclusive-minded persons who have traditionally been marginalized by public institutions is now being matched and/or surpassed by other groups, some of them extremist groups, that have very different goals in mind. For example, a visceral fear, particularly voiced by some conservative White parents, that their identity and culture are being ignored or erased is prompting efforts to ban books, eliminate positions responsible for promoting diversity and equity, outlaw critical race theory, and limit the discussion of race and LGBTQ+ issues—all in direct opposition to inclusion. These conflicting viewpoints, particularly those borne of extremist movements, have sparked verbal fireworks at countless public gatherings in recent years.

Regardless of the person or group making demands, the courageous leader must first validate and affirm the emotions and feelings that people are bringing into conversations and meetings. Humanity must be honored at all times. When courageous leaders start a dialogue or respond to a statement by modeling the appropriate validation and affirmation of humanity, they send a strong message of inclusivity to all. This validation also goes far in establishing a culture that is conducive to constructive conversations. To validate and affirm, courageous leaders will often meet resistance and challenging conversations with words and stems such as:

"I respect your. . . . "

"I appreciate. . . . "

"I can relate to. . . . "

"I recognize. . . . "

"I love how. . . . "

"I honor. . . . "

"I see you. . . . "

"I hear you. . . . "

After the needed validation and affirmation of the participants—regardless of their beliefs, perspective, and/or lived experience—professional educators and courageous leaders must then shift to facilitating a learning experience. This happens through the sharing of research, data, stories, and other information that provide the needed scholarship and context to engage in constructive and collaborative conversations. Many people come to public meetings already laden with, and in reaction to, misconceptions and misinformation. Providing clear, reliable, and fact-based information may dispel at least a portion of some participants' fear and defensive anger that have accumulated as a response to feeling unheard and disrespected.

Other ways to build mental models may involve the illumination of existing practices and policies that have perpetuated exclusion and oppression. Building common understanding and bridging information and knowledge gaps among all parties are important steps toward sustainable change. However, leaders may not always have an immediate solution in mind for the complex problems. For this reason, tone-setting and relationships established through the initial validation and affirmation process are crucial to cultivating future agreements in the face of cultural differences.

In no way are these steps meant to imply that hateful and disruptive comments in public meetings can be quickly soothed or quelled by a few strategies of communication. If only it were so simple. However, given the increasing instances of hate-driven behavior in communities across this nation, doing nothing is not an option. Extremism is insidious and feeds on rumors, disinformation, and fear. It can infect our families, friends, colleagues, and neighbors—to say nothing of the political leaders whose decisions affect our daily lives. That is why each of us must dig deep within ourselves and find the courage to stand up for common decency and democratic values. Learning how to have civil and meaningful dialogues in our own town halls, PTA meetings, and places of worship is a worthy and productive place to start.

## PROACTIVE COMMUNICATION

For educators, there is an important lesson to be learned from the current confrontation with extremism. Extremist groups have taken advantage of the public's lack of understanding of school initiatives that promote diversity, equity, and inclusion or culturally responsive pedagogy or social-emotional learning. One of the significant weaknesses of our public school systems is the lack of focus on communications in general, as well as on strong parent and community partnerships.

Until recently, it has been rare for school districts other than large urban school districts or districts in affluent communities to have staff specifically devoted to communications. And even when school districts have a designated communications position or department, it is typically one or two staff members who largely focus on crisis communication, management of the district's website and social media accounts, regular newsletters, and specific superintendent and board communications.

In general, school districts have not broadly disseminated detailed information on the rationale behind specific initiatives for the purpose of educating the public and garnering support for these initiatives. Parents and the community need to understand why particular programs are important to student success and staff effectiveness. They also need to understand what these programs look like in the classroom as experienced by students. Too often, because the rationale for an initiative like inclusion or social-emotional learning seems self-evident to educators, school leaders don't take the time to elaborate on that rationale for parents and community members in order to ensure people understand and are supportive of these programs.

As mentioned in chapter 7, when first attacked for teaching critical race theory and social-emotional learning in the Virginia Beach City schools, Superintendent Aaron Spence realized that many parents, community members, and even staff weren't aware of what the district was doing and why. The consequence was that some people mistook culturally responsive approaches to instruction as critical race theory and believed the false claim that social-emotional learning was a Trojan horse for critical race theory. Once Spence realized the gap in understanding, the district launched a significant communications initiative—not only with parents and community groups but also with staff—so that everyone heard a common message and understood the rationale and importance of culturally responsive approaches and social-emotional learning.

When a school or district understands the importance of communication and takes an active role in building understanding among staff, parents, and the community, the impact is broader than people simply knowing why the district is engaging in a particular practice. Staff, parents, and community members become communicators themselves, reaching out to friends and neighbors in support of district initiatives. And when controversy emerges, they are there to share their understanding and support. The best guarantee of resistance to extremism is the support of the district's constituents.

At the national level, only recently did numerous organizations involved in working on such issues as equity and social-emotional learning become acutely aware of the need for effective communication with parents and community members to bring clarity to what these concepts mean, how they can positively impact students, and why they are important for the overall success of instruction in academic content. For example, the Collaborative for Academic, Social, and Emotional Learning (CASEL) was joined by more than thirty associations—including such major national associations for superintendents and administrators as AASA, ASCD, the National Association of Elementary School Principals (NAESP), and the National Association of Secondary School Principals (NASSP)—in a coalition designed to educate parents and the public about the value of social-emotional learning. The coalition, entitled Leading with SEL, produced toolkits for educating parents and school board members and reached out to media sources to ensure that the strong evidence supporting social-emotional learning was getting through to the general public and to parents.

In an era when social media can rapidly disseminate both misinformation and disinformation, schools and school districts have to engage in proactive and two-way communication. They need to not only educate parents about initiatives and strategies they are using to reach particular students but also provide parents and the community with opportunities to raise questions and understand these programs more deeply. At a time when the technology available to districts has evolved so that district and school leaders can quickly access the perspectives of parents and community members, it is essential that districts seek this input and devote time and resources to effective two-way communication.

Two-way communication can be as simple as enabling people to respond to questions from the district such as, "Was this program description helpful in understanding its importance for our students?" and "After reading this, what questions do you still have that you would like answered?" In other cases, focus groups and forums can bring valuable information to the school or district in order to help more people understand the direction the district is taking, the meaningfulness of programs, and the projected impact the programs will have.

Engaging parents and community members in goal setting or strategic planning prior to the launch of an initiative can help to refine the direction the initiative is taking, improve its effectiveness, and garner broad community support. In the same way, engaging staff in the planning process and leadership of initiatives grounds those programs in support from the people who will be implementing them. There are numerous strategies for promoting proactive, two-way communication, but what is most important is that educators recognize it as an essential aspect of any new initiative.

Admittedly, proactive and two-way communication won't prevent all extremist attacks on district programs. However, it will provide a buffer of well-informed parents and community members who can come to the assistance of the district when conflict emerges over important programs.

## ROOT CAUSES OF DIVISIVENESS—FEAR AND THREAT

If we are to address the divisiveness within our current culture, we have to realize that much of the divisiveness stems from fear. Individuals with extremist views have promoted and escalated that fear by communicating to people, particularly White people, that they are losing the primacy of their social standing as America's society becomes more diverse. They also have engendered fear among parents that their children are being educated in a way that will lead them to become gay or transgender, or to hold religious and political beliefs strikingly different from those of their parents, or to feel responsible for and guilty of perpetrating past injustices in the history of the country and, as an outgrowth of any of these, to accept a "woke" ideology.

Extremist groups have been effective in convincing many concerned parents that education is indoctrination and that they have to choose whether they want that indoctrination to be in right-wing values, often framed as traditional values, or in leftist values, often framed by individuals with extremist views as radical or socialist values. These parents are made to feel under threat of having their children taken from them socially and emotionally, if not physically. Once people experience this barrage of manufactured fear, they are prone to react by publicly translating it into anger at those who are perceived as presenting the threat.

To bolster their contention that education is indoctrination, extremist groups have begun to label public schools as "government" schools in order to communicate that these schools indoctrinate children into valuing big government and leftist values about the benefits of government. This view is seen as in opposition to the freedom provided by "private" schools, which allow parents to indoctrinate children with the values that parents hold because parents have a choice in which schools their children attend.

These strategies for creating fear and threat are not new. They have been used by demagogues and authoritarians throughout the ages. And many people who already feel vulnerable fall prey to these propaganda tactics. Others, who perhaps are opposed to the tactics and goals of extremist groups, fall silent for fear of retaliation.

To move away from divisiveness, we have to address these fears directly by helping people recognize that public education is antithetical to indoctrination. The goal of public education is to help young people develop independence of thought through understanding multiple perspectives and making judgments based on accurate historical and scientific evidence. The goal is also to complicate students' thinking so that they won't accept simple, and often wrong, answers to complex problems. At the same time, while public schools are anti-indoctrination, they are not neutral with regard to commonly accepted democratic values and principles such as opposing prejudice, discrimination, and injustice.

Understanding that education is diametrically opposed to indoctrination may be particularly challenging for those whose beliefs are based on myths and conspiracy theories. But for most people, enabling children to think critically, creatively, and independently means that they are more likely to be successful in whatever career or vocation they pursue. Although their ideas and assumptions may be challenged by hearing the perspective of others or by learning historical and scientific truths, that exposure enables them to grow as individuals and contribute more effectively as engaged citizens in our democracy.

In order for schools to foster independence of thought, they need to be safe places where all students feel comfortable taking the learning risks necessary to grow. This means that all students, no matter their background, race, religion, political orientation, or gender orientation, need to feel known, valued, cared about, and respected. The history of education in the United States has been the story of ever-more-inclusive environments. That story is far from finished; schools must continue to grow in inclusiveness as we more deeply understand the diversity of racial, ethnic, religious, and gender identities among us. Schools should be identity-safe places for all students. Policies and practices that promote caring, safe, and inclusive environments are critical to enabling the personal and academic growth of each student. As Aaron Spence opined in his op-ed to the Virginia Beach City community, "Surely, we can all agree on that."

The politicization of education reduces education into a binary right-versus-left debate when, in fact, it is neither right nor left. When educators speak to the importance of equity, it is to guarantee the academic success of all children, not to elevate some while diminishing others. When educators speak to the importance of diversity and cultural responsiveness, it is to ensure that children from all backgrounds feel at home in their schools, not to undermine the value of the cultures White children bring to school. When educators talk about inclusion, it is to ensure that all students feel known, valued, and appreciated for who they are and the assets they bring with them to school. And when educators speak of social-emotional learning, it is to create classroom and school environments that are most productive for student learning and to enable young people to work together well.

These aren't political or cultural agendas but central conditions for learning and for the success of children in school. In fact, the reason school board elections were established as nonpartisan and as primarily focused on the well-being and positive development of all children was to depoliticize education for the inclusion of all in the schoolhouse.

Public education is a disruptor. It disrupts ignorance by attending to the examination of historical, scientific, and societal evidence. The pursuit of truth, the pursuit of expanding our understanding of the world around us, and the pursuit of being effective in the world are the essential goals of education. It is not about adopting a "woke" or a "right-wing" ideology. It's the examination of ideology itself so that we can make independent, evidenced-based, compassionate, and thoughtful judgments.

To address the fears about public education that have been stoked by individuals with extremist views and extremist groups, we have to overcome our own fears of the consequences of speaking out and recenter the conversation back to education's essential goals within a democratic society. Education in authoritarian and totalitarian societies is about indoctrination in which only certain facts, evidence, theories, and perspectives are allowed, and often certain races, ethnicities, or cultures are viewed as superior to others. Education in a democratic and pluralistic society accepts the equality and humanity of all individuals and considers many political and social perspectives in order to introduce young people to the diversity of views they will need to consider as citizens who have to make important participatory decisions in a democratic society. The fabric woven by this diversity of ideas, cultures, and backgrounds is a necessary ingredient for sustaining our democratic nation.

To move away from divisiveness, we need to have the courage to speak about and act on those core principles of education in a democratic society. We need to clearly call out extremist strategies for the disinformation they present and the false fears they ignite.

We need to work collectively to reclaim the vital role that public education serves in a democratic society. And we need to restore our own confidence that we can model for students ways of working together that appreciate difference, value each individual, and support success for all.

Together, we can achieve these goals if we have the courage to stand up, speak out, and act on our beliefs. If we wish to achieve quality education for our children and create a more just, safe, democratic, and compassionate society, standing up is not a choice; it's the requisite first step in moving forward.

# Epilogue

It is understandable that in times of social conflict we may hesitate to step forward. We may have a fear, perhaps grounded in reality, of being attacked by those who oppose our views. Such attacks do not have to be physical to constitute a viable threat. Instead, they may consist of false or misleading statements spread on social media or the relatively recent strategy of doxing. Given that digital communication has become such an essential element of our daily lives, these and other online intrusions can have an immediate and chilling effect on our good intentions to speak up against words or deeds that menace the democratic role of education.

We may also think to ourselves, "I'm only one person. What difference can I make?" The gravity and extent of today's social disinformation can effectively paralyze us, making the challenges appear so vast and insurmountable that we retreat into our more comfortable environment rather than take the risk of righting a wrong or preventing a misdeed.

When the possibility of threats leaves us figuratively quaking in fear, perhaps we should remember the lessons of the Pando. The Pando is a forest in Utah that covers over one hundred acres. What's so unusual about that, you ask? The uniqueness of the Pando springs from its source—one lone quaking aspen. The Pando forest is actually a single tree that has spread through its underground root structure over the span of about 10,000 years or longer. Some of this quaking aspen's shoots now tower 80 feet high, and the Pando is recognized as one of the largest living organisms on earth.

At the risk of sounding anthropomorphic, we encourage you to consider the life of this tree. For centuries, it has fended off threats both natural and human-made, from lightning to hungry herbivores to encroaching development. At the same time, it has spread its message underground, producing hundreds of sprouts that now stand tall and convey the founding tree's message of strength in its purpose and pride in its mission.

We can find resolve, courage, and inspiration in this singular quaking aspen, which ignores its genetically induced trembling to carry on its work and safeguard its future. Rather than be overwhelmed by the potential dangers that surround it, the Pando focuses each day on making a meaningful difference in its one corner of the world. We would do well to follow its example.

—Joyce A. Barnes, editor and contributor

# References

Andover Public Schools. (2015). *Group norms and agreements* [Unpublished manuscript from working group].

Anthony, C. E., Lee, T., Gottlieb, J., & Rainwater, B. (2021). *On the frontlines of today's cities: Trauma, challenges and solutions.* National League of Cities. https://www.nlc.org/wp-content/uploads/2021/11/On-the-Frontlines-of-Todays-Cities-1.pd

Anti-Defamation League Center on Extremism. (February 2023). *Murder and extremism in the United States in 2022.* https://www.adl.org/resources/report/murder-and-extremism-united-states-2022

Associated Press. (August 18, 2023). Six Arkansas schools to offer African American AP course despite restrictions. *Guardian.* https://www.theguardian.com/us-news/2023/aug/18/arkansas-high-school-african-american-studies-ap-course

Balu, A. (June 15, 2023). Emily LaBar and Jacob Cruz: Pushing school boards on LGBTQ+ rights. *Pod Virginia.* https://podvirginia.com/pod-blog/emily-labar-and-jacob-cruz-pushing-school-boards-on-lgbtq-rights

Beauchamp, Z. (September 10, 2023). Chris Rufo's dangerous fictions. *Vox.* https://www.vox.com/23811277/christopher-rufo-culture-wars-ron-desantis-florida-critical-race-theory-anti-wokeness

Berman, S. (1985). *A comparison of dialogue and debate* [Unpublished manuscript based on discussions of the Dialogue Group of the Boston Chapter of Educators for Social Responsibility].

———. (1997). *Children's social consciousness and the development of social responsibility. Albany, NY:* SUNY Press.

———. (2023). *Implementing social-emotional learning: Insights from districts' successes and setbacks.* Lanham, MD: Rowman & Littlefield.

Berwick, C. (August 9, 2019). Is it time to detrack math? *Edutopia.* https://www.edutopia.org/article/it-time-detrack-math/

Black, D. (2011). Voluntary desegregation, resegregation, and the hope for equal educational opportunity. American Bar Association, *Human Rights Magazine, 38*(2). https://www.americanbar.org/groups/crsj/publications/human_rights_magazine_home/human_rights_vol38_2011/fall2011/voluntary _desegregation_resegregation_and_the_hope_for_equal_educational _opportunity/

Bohrnstedt, G., Kitmitto, S., Ogut, B., Sherman, D., & Chan, D. (2015). *School composition and the Black-White achievement gap*. National Center for Education Statistics, NCES 2015–018.

Briscoe, JJ. (September 19, 2023). School board changes can destroy students' educational opportunities. We're paying attention. *Kansas Reflector*. https://kansasreflector.com/2023/09/19/school-board-changes-can-destroy-students-educational-opportunities-were-paying-attention/

Butts, R. F. (1980). *The revival of civic learning: A rationale for citizenship education in American schools*. Phi Delta Kappa.

Carr, N. (May 13, 2023). The student protesters were arrested. The man who got violent in the parking lot wasn't. *ProPublica*. https://www.propublica.org/article/conway-arkansas-school-board-high-school-arrests

———. (May 20, 2023). He became convinced the school board was pushing "transgender bullshit." He ended up arrested—and emboldened. *ProPublica*. https://www.propublica.org/article/winston-salem-nc-school-board-arrests

Cavallaro, M. M. How Black moms in Temecula are fighting the school board's right-wing takeover. (October 31, 2023). *The Nation*. https://www.thenation.com/article/society/temecula-california-school-board-recall-election/

Chait, J. (May 8, 2023). Indoctrination nation: Convinced that schools are brainwashing kids to be left-wingers, conservatives are seizing control of the American classroom. *Intelligencer*. https://nymag.com/intelligencer/article/desantis-florida-trump-education-politics.html

Clary, E. G., & Miller, J. (1986). Socialization and situational influences on sustained altruism. *Child Development, 57*(6), 1358–69.

Colby, A., & Damon, W. (1992). *Some do care*. Free Press.

courage. (2024). *Merriam-Webster.com*.

Cullum, J. (July 25, 2023). ACPS ignores Gov. Youngkin's recommended policies on treatment of transgender students. *ALX Now*. https://www.alxnow.com/2023/07/25/acps-ignores-gov-youngkins-recommended-policies-restricting-transgender-students/

Daloz, L. A. P., Keen, C. H., Keen, J. P., & Parks, S. D. (1996). *Common fire: Leading lives of commitment in a complex world*. Beacon Press.

Dana, J. (February 20, 2023). Parents defend Scottsdale superintendent who AZ legislators want fired. [Video interview]. 12News KPNX-TV. https://www.12news.com/article/news/local/valley/scottsdale-parents-defend-superintendent/75-a45e6975-e6d0-4539-8355-c72409606243

Day, J., Khan, A., & Loadenthal, M. (October 2022). *Threats and harassment against local officials dataset*. Princeton University's Bridging Divides

Initiative. https://bridgingdivides.princeton.edu/sites/g/files/toruqf246/files/documents/Threats%20and%20Harassment%20Report.pdf

Derksen, C. (August 22, 2023). Ryan Walters labels Oklahoma librarian's video an example of "woke agenda" in Twitter firestorm. *Oklahoman.* https://www.oklahoman.com/story/news/education/2023/08/22/ryan-walters-tweet-librarian-featured-ellen-degeneres/70652781007/

Doherty, C., Kiley, J., Asheer, N., & Price, T. (2022). As partisan hostility grows, signs of frustration with the two-party system. *Pew U.S. Politics and Policy,* 1–78. https://www.pewresearch.org/politics/2022/08/09/as-partisan-hostility-grows-signs-of-frustration-with-the-two-party-system/

Eaton, S., & Chirichigno, G. (2011). *The impact of racially diverse schools in a democratic society. Research Brief No. 3. Updated.* National Coalition on School Diversity. https://files.eric.ed.gov/fulltext/ED571627.pdf

Education Trust–New York. (October 2017). *See our truth: The state of teacher and school leader diversity in New York, and why it matters for students, educators, and our future.* https://seeourtruth-ny.edtrust.org/wp-content/uploads/sites/4/2017/10/See-Our-Truth.pdf

Elordi, M. (July 27, 2023). Some Virginia school districts bucking governor's policies on transgender bathrooms, pronouns. *Daily Wire.* https://www.dailywire.com/news/some-virginia-school-districts-bucking-governors-policies-on-transgender-bathrooms-pronouns

Erikson, E. H. (1968). *Identity: Youth and crisis.* W. W. Norton.

Florida Department of Education. (2023). *Florida's state academic standards—Social studies, 2023.* https://www.fldoe.org/core/fileparse.php/20653/urlt/6-4.pdf

Frankenberg, E., Garces, L. M., & Hopkins, M. (Eds.). (2016). *School integration matters: Research-based strategies to advance equity.* New York: Teachers College Press.

Friedman, J., & Tager, J. (November 2021). *Educational gag orders: Legislative restrictions on the freedom to read, learn, and teach.* PEN America. https://pen.org/report/educational-gag-orders/

Gluckman, N. (February 2, 2023). "This is how censorship happens": How vague laws and heightened fears are creating a repressive climate on campus. *Chronicle of Higher Education.* www.chronicle.com/article/is-this-how-censorship-happens

Golden, D. (January 3, 2023). Muzzled by DeSantis, critical race theory professors cancel courses or modify their teaching. *ProPublica.* https://www.propublica.org/article/desantis-critical-race-theory-florida-college-professors

Goodwin, G. E. (May 9, 2023). A Colorado school board was taken over by Trump-loving conservatives. Now nearly half its high-school teachers are bailing. *Business Insider.* https://www.insider.com/colorado-school-district-taken-over-conservatives-driving-away-teachers-2023-5

Greenberg, M. (2023). Evidence for social and emotional learning in schools. Learning Policy Institute. https://doi.org/10.54300/928.269

Grossman, H. (February 6, 2023). Radical-left superintendent in fiery political turmoil after "racist views" against White people exposed. Fox News. https://www.foxnews.com/media/radical-left-superintendent-fiery-political-turmoil-racist-views-against-white-people-exposed

Hale, J. N. (2021). *The choice we face: How segregation, race, and power have shaped America's most controversial education reform movement.* Beacon Press.

Hanna, M. (October 21, 2023). Pennridge ordered to produce library records, pay legal fees for dad challenging book removals. *Philadelphia Inquirer.* https://www.inquirer.com/education/pennridge-school-district-book-ban-lawsuit-darren-laustsen-20231021.html

Hawkins, B. (August 30, 2023). Of rules & law: Virginia's largest school districts won't adopt Gov. Youngkin's new LGBTQ edict. *The 74.* https://www.the74million.org/article/of-rules-law-virginias-largest-districts-wont-adopt-new-state-lgbt-edict/

Hoehn, R. A. (1983). *Up from apathy: A study of moral and social involvement.* Abingdon.

Horowitz, J. (October 26, 2022). *Parents differ sharply by party over what their K–12 children should learn in school.* Pew Research Center. https://www.pewresearch.org/social-trends/2022/10/26/parents-differ-sharply-by-party-over-what-their-k-12-children-should-learn-in-school/

Jefferson County Public Schools. (2008). *No retreat: JCPS commitment to school desegregation* [Out of print].

Jennings, T. E. (1992). *Self-in-connection as a component of human-rights advocacy* [Unpublished manuscript].

Johnson, R. C., & Nazaryan, R. (2019). *Children of the dream: Why school integration works.* Basic Books.

Jones, A. (July 19, 2022). July 19th public library board meeting public comments. *Speaking Out.* https://sites.google.com/view/abmack33/speaking-out?authuser=0

Keniston, K. (1968). *Young radicals: Notes on committed youth.* Harcourt, Brace & World.

Kidder, R. W. (2005). *Moral courage: Taking action when your values are put to the test.* Harper.

Kiel, D. (2010). Accepting Justice Kennedy's dare: The future of integration in a post-PICS world. *Fordham Law Review, 78*(6), 2873–2917. https://core.ac.uk/download/pdf/144228899.pdf

King Jr., M. L. (2012). *A gift of love: Sermons from "Strength to Love" and other preachings.* Beacon Press.

Kopan, T. (August 10, 2023). Teacher of the year was supposed to be an honor. Then politics intervened. *Boston Globe.* https://www.bostonglobe.com/2023/08/10/nation/teacher-of-the-year-culture-wars/

Kreisberg, S. (1992). *Transforming power: Domination, empowerment, and education.* Albany, NY: SUNY Press.

Laustsen, D. (June 29, 2023). In Pennridge School District, books once shadow banned are now in the trash can. *Bucks County Beacon.* https://buckscountybeacon.com/2023/06/in-pennridge-school-district-books-once-shadow-banned-are-now-in-the-trash-can/

Lee, G. (2006). *Courage: The backbone of leadership.* Hoboken, NJ: Jossey-Bass.

Liautaud, S. (2021). *The power of ethics: How to make good choices in a complicated world.* New York: Simon & Schuster.

Locke, R., & Luna, C. (2023). "How scared are you?": Mapping the threat environment of San Diego's elected officials. *Kroc IPJ Research and Resources,* 68. https://digital.sandiego.edu/ipj-research/68

Marcotte, A. (October 10, 2023). Moms for Liberty meets its match: Parents in this swing suburban district are fighting back. *Salon.* https://www.salon.com/2023/10/10/moms-for-liberty-meets-its-match-parents-in-this-swing-suburban-district-are-fighting-back/

———. (November 9, 2023). "I'm so tired of these psychos": Moms for Liberty is now a toxic brand. *Salon.* https://www.salon.com/2023/11/09/im-so-tired-of-these-psychos-moms-for-liberty-is-now-a-brand/

Mickelson, R. A., & Nkomo, M. (2012). Integrated schooling, life course outcomes, and social cohesion in multiethnic democratic societies. *Review of Research in Education, 36*(1), 197–238.

Moms for Liberty. (n.d.) *Social emotional learning: Guide for parents.* https://portal.momsforliberty.org/media/files/files/b0d67d1f/sel-packet-120622-0845-2-.pdf

Moss, L., & LaRoue, J. (June 14, 2023). VB school board narrowly adopts LGBTQ+ resolution. *10WAVY.* https://www.wavy.com/news/local-news/virginia-beach/vb-school-board-debates-lgbtq-resolution/

Natanson, H. (March 6, 2023). "Slavery was wrong" and 5 other things some educators won't teach anymore. *Washington Post.* www.washingtonpost.com/education/2023/03/06/slavery-was-wrong-5-other-things-educators-wont-teach-anymore/

National Center for Education Statistics. (2010). *National Assessment of Educational Progress (NAEP): Trial urban district assessment reading 2009.*

———. (October, 2022). *2022 NAEP mathematics assessment: Highlighted results at grades 4 and 8 for the nation, states, and districts.* https://nces.ed.gov/pubsearch/pubsinfo.asp?pubid=2022124

National Constitution Center. (2024). Supreme Court Case: Engel v. Vitale, 370 U.S. 421 (1962). Excerpt: Majority Opinion: Justice Hugo Black. National Constitution Center. https://constitutioncenter.org/the-constitution/supreme-court-case-library/engel-v-vitale

National Council of Supervisors of Mathematics and TODOS: Mathematics for All. (2016). *Mathematics education through the lens of social*

*justice: Acknowledgment, actions, and accountability.* https://www.todos
-math.org/assets/docs2016/2016Enews/3.pospaper16_wtodos_8pp.pdf

Nelson, S. (October 12, 2022). Oceanside Unified recognized as LGBTQ supportive school district. *Coast News.* https://thecoastnews.com/oceanside
-unified-recognized-as-lgbtq-supportive-school-district/

———. (February 10, 2023). Community clashes over LGBTQ
books in Oceanside schools. *Coast News.* https://thecoastnews
.com/community-clashes-over-lgbtq-books-in-oceanside
-schools/#: ~: text=Vitale%2C%20a%20member%20of%20the
,supportive%20school%20by%20Equality%20California

Nin, A. (1969). *The diary of Anaïs Nin: Volume 3, 1939–1944.* Harcourt Brace
Jovanovich.

Oceanside Unified School District. (June 14, 2022). *OUSD Board of Education
meeting: June 14, 2022* [Video]. YouTube. https://www.youtube.com/
watch?v=q_fsNtADuYo

———. (February 7, 2023). *OUSD Board of Education meeting: February 7, 2023*
[Video]. YouTube. https://www.youtube.com/watch?v=BIB0zYv3FZY

Oliner, S., & Oliner, P. (1988). *The altruistic personality: Rescuers of Jews in Nazi
Europe.* Free Press.

Pettigrew, T. F., & Tropp, L. R. (2006). A meta-analytic test of intergroup contact
theory. *Journal of Personality and Social Psychology, 90*(5), 751.

Petrilli, M. (May 27, 2021). The common ground on race and education that's
hiding in plain sight. *Flypaper.* Thomas B. Fordham Institute. https:
//fordhaminstitute.org/national/commentary/common-ground-race-and
-education-thats-hiding-plain-sight

Pollock, M., & Rogers, J. (January 2022). *The conflict campaign: Exploring local
experiences of the campaign to ban "critical race theory" in public K–12 education in the U.S., 2020–2021.* UCLA Institute for Democracy, Education, and Access. https://idea.gseis.ucla.edu/publications/the-conflict
-campaign/publications/files/the-conflict-campaign-report

Prince William County Public Schools. (August 17, 2023). PWCS policy
738 nondiscrimination and harassment of students, remains in effect.
Prince William County Public Schools. https://www.pwcs.edu/news/2023
/08/nondiscrimination_policy

Rabinove, S. (1988). Church and state must remain separate. In J. S. Bach (Ed.),
*Civil liberties: Opposing viewpoints* (p. 55). New York: Greenhaven Press.

Rahman, K. (November 9, 2023). Moms for Liberty annihilated in school board
elections. *Newsweek.* https://www.newsweek.com/moms-liberty-school
-board-elections-1842225

Reardon, S. F. (September 2016). School segregation and racial academic
achievement gaps. *Russell Sage Foundation Journal of the Social Sciences,
2*(5), 34–57.

Reardon, S. F., & Owens, A. (2014). 60 years after *Brown*: Trends and consequences of school segregation. *Annual Review of Sociology, 40*, 199–218.

RIDGE Network. (n.d.). The story of the RIDGE Network. About Us. https://www.ridgenetwork.org/blank-1

Ritter, S. (September 16, 2022). "Outraged": Johnson County students walk out of class over transgender bathroom policy. *Kansas City Star*. https://www.kansascity.com/news/local/education/article265805621.html

Rogers, J., & Kahne, J. with Ishimoto, M., Kwako, A., Stern, S. C., Bingener, C., Raphael, L., Alkam, S., & Conde, Y. (2022). *Educating for a diverse democracy: The chilling role of political conflict in blue, purple, and red communities*. Los Angeles, CA: UCLA's Institute for Democracy, Education, and Access.

Rosenhan, D. L. (1972). Learning theory and prosocial behavior. *Journal of Social Issues, 28*(3), 151–64.

Rowan, L. (November 13, 2023). "I'm not safe here": This teenager won't stop advocating for LGBTQ+ students in Roanoke County. *Cardinal News*. https://cardinalnews.org/2023/11/13/im-not-safe-here-this-teenager-wont-stop-advocating-for-lgbtq-students-in-roanoke-county/

Schwartz, S. (August 31, 2023). PragerU, creator of controversial social studies videos, now has a toehold in schools. *Education Week*. https://www.edweek.org/teaching-learning/prageru-creator-of-controversial-social-studies-videos-now-has-a-toehold-in-schools/2023/08#:~:text=Despite%20having%20"U"%20in%20the,%2C%20media%2C%20and%20education

Shah, N. (August 18, 2023). Arkansas schools will teach AP African American studies despite state's objection. *USA Today*. https://www.usatoday.com/story/news/education/2023/08/18/arkansas-schools-will-teach-ap-african-american-studies/70617810007/

Shernuk, P. (October 18, 2023). Schools and school boards shape Kansas communities. Here's why I stay involved. *Kansas Reflector*. https://kansasreflector.com/2023/10/18/schools-and-school-boards-shape-kansas-communities-heres-why-i-stay-involved/

Smith, T. (August 11, 2023). The plot thickens: The battle over books comes at a cost. *All Things Considered*, NPR. https://www.npr.org/2023/08/11/1192034923/the-plot-thickens-the-battle-over-books-comes-at-a-cost

Spence, A. (July 3, 2021). Lower the temperature of critical race theory debate. *Virginian-Pilot*. https://www.pilotonline.com/2021/07/03/aaron-spence-lower-the-temperature-of-critical-race-theory-debate/

Sterbenz, C. (September 1, 2023). How we fight back: Library workers and advocates are turning to new policies, lawsuits, and legislation to stem the tide of book bans. *American Libraries Magazine*. https://americanlibrariesmagazine.org/2023/09/01/how-we-fight-back/

Strauss, V. (August 10, 2023). Florida says it doesn't want indoctrination in schools—but look at the materials it just approved. *Washington Post.* https://www.washingtonpost.com/education/2023/08/10/indoctrination-florida-approves-schools/

Suliman, A. (August 19, 2023). Georgia teacher fired after reading book on gender to fifth-grade class. *Washington Post.* https://www.washingtonpost.com/nation/2023/08/19/georgia-teacher-katie-rinderle-fired-book/

Tegeler, P., Mickelson, R. A., & Bottia, M. (2011). *What we know about school integration, college attendance, and the reduction of poverty. Research Brief No. 4. Updated.* National Coalition on School Diversity. https://files.eric.ed.gov/fulltext/ED571628.pdf

Tyner, A. (2021). *How to sell SEL: Parents and the politics of social-emotional learning.* Thomas B. Fordham Institute. https://fordhaminstitute.org/sites/default/files/publication/pdfs/20210811-how-sell-sel-parents-and-politics-social-emotional-learning826.pdf

United States Department of Justice–Civil Rights Division & United States Department of Education–Office of Civil Rights. (2011). *Guidance on the voluntary use of race to achieve diversity and avoid racial isolation in elementary and secondary schools.* https://www2.ed.gov/about/offices/list/ocr/docs/guidance-ese-201111.html

United States Department of Justice–Office of Public Affairs. (October 4, 2021). *Justice Department addresses violent threats against school officials and teachers.* Press release. https://www.justice.gov/opa/pr/justice-department-addresses-violent-threats-against-school-officials-and-teachers

Virginia Department of Education. (2023). Model policies on ensuring privacy, dignity, and respect for all students and parents in Virginia's Public Schools. https://www.doe.virginia.gov/parents-students/for-parents/model-policies-on-ensuring-privacy-dignity-and-respect-for-all-students-and-parents-in-virginia-s-public-schools

Wiesel, E. (October 10, 1986). Nobel Peace Prize Acceptance Speech. The Nobel Foundation. Reprinted in *Night*, E. Wiesel, translated 2006. New York: Hill and Wang.

Woo, A., Lee, S., Prado Tuma, A., Kaufman, J. H., Lawrence, R. A., & Reed, N. (2023). *Walking on eggshells—Teachers' responses to classroom limitations on race- or gender-related topics: Findings from the 2022 American Instructional Resources Survey.* Santa Monica, CA: RAND. www.rand.org/pubs/research_reports/RRA134-16.html

Woo, A., Wolfe, R. L., Steiner, E. D., Doan, S., Lawrence, R. A., Berdie, L., Greer, L., Gittens, A. D., & Schwartz, H. L. (2022). *Walking a fine line—Educators' views on politicized topics in schooling: Findings from the State of the American Teacher and State of the American Principal Surveys.* Santa Monica, CA: RAND. www.rand.org/pubs/research_reports/RRA1108-5.html

Wu, W. (February 8, 2023). Disastrous learning results, ideological indoctrination prompt working-class, military community to speak up. *California Globe.* https://californiaglobe.com/fr/disastrous-learning-results-ideological-indoctrination-prompt-working-class-military-community-to-speak-up/

Young, J. C., Friedman, J., & Meehan, K. (November 9, 2023). *America's censored classrooms 2023.* PEN America. https://pen.org/report/americas-censored-classrooms-2023/

Youniss, J., and Yates, M. (1999). Youth service and moral-civic identity: A case for everyday morality. *Educational Psychology Review, 11,* 361–76.

Zalaznick, M. (July 26, 2023). Virginia superintendents line up to defy new K12 transgender restrictions. *District Administration.* https://districtadministration.com/superintendents-k12-leaders-defy-virginia-transgender-student-model-policies/

## CREDIT

Portions of chapter 7 were drawn, with permission of editor Jay Goldman, from:

Berman, S. (February 2023). Reclaiming the narrative. *School Administrator, 80(2),* 24–27. https://www.pageturnpro.com/AASA/107489-February-2023/sdefault.html#page/26

# INDEX

through leadership, 117–18;
McCarthyism faced with,
16; moral strength in, 32;
not one-and-done, 140;
perseverance of, 6; personal
quality of, 2–3, 69–70;
requirements for, 138–39;
social justice fight with
personal, 12–14; speaking
out with, 163; standing up
with, 109–10; sustained and
active efforts in, 138–40
COVID-19 pandemic, 115
Cramer, Jane, 134, 137
crisis-in-courage moment, 92
critical race theory, 26, 51,
53, 96, 112; conservative
politics targeting, 56;
Sanders banning, 119;
school board banning, 50
critical thinking, 33–34,
160–61
Cruz, Jay, 130–33, 140
Cullen, Joan, 134
cultures, 35, 40
culture wars, 19–20, 127–28

Dahmer, Vernon, 19
Daloz, L. A. P., 61, 64–66, 141
Damon, W., 61, 63, 65
debates: dialogue compared to,
147–51, *148–49*; once you
defend you're losing in, 105
defending, you're losing if, 105

DEI. *See* Diversity, Equity, and
Inclusion
democracy: accountability
in, 99; antidemocratic
proposals in, 33; censorship
in, 103; children sustaining,
42; diversity in, 97;
education's importance in,
27; governance of, 41–44;
pluralistic society in, 23;
public education sustaining,
41, 43, 163; public
education with principles
of, 2; sustaining, 15–16; as
vulnerable, 139
Department of Justice, 49
desegregation, 86;
communities experiencing,
85; of Louisville
Independent School
District, 84–85; students
attending schools with,
83–84; students benefiting
from, 87
destructive behavior, 146
dialogue: common ground
sought in, 151; debate
compared to, 147–51,
*148–49*; facilitating, 150–
51; multiple perspectives
welcomed in, 153–54; skills
developed for, 151–52
DiAngelo, Robin, 121–22

equity, 96, 123–24; academic,
7; for common ground,
103; in education, 13;
educational access
with, 93–94; fairness or
impartiality in, 70; in school
districts, 71; in social justice,
71; strategies for, 79–80; for
students, 80
Erikson, Erik, 64
Ervin, Sam, 39
escape routes, 10
ethical considerations, 42
ethical leaders, 31–32
ethnicity, 35–36
Evers, Medgar, 19
extremism: far-left liberal
bias and, 27; historical
discrimination ignored in,
25–26; public education
attacked by, 24; in United
States, 23. *See also* right-
wing extremism
extremist groups: anti-
government, 115–16; DEI
elimination goal of, 134;
Moms for Liberty as, 53,
116–17; "parents' rights"
catchphrase of, 24–25;
public schools labeled by,
159–60; Vermilion as, 135
extremist views: educators
targeted by, 51–53; hatred
in, 98–99; insidious nature

of, 155–56; people running
against, 137–38; political
indoctrination in, 43; public
education fears stoked by,
162; school board members
with, 112–15, 120–28;
in school boards, 49–50;
school boards taken over by,
53–54; speaking out against,
99–100; students against,
129–30; winning by any
means with, 97–98

facts, 22
fairness, 70
family business, 9–11
family history, 4
far-left liberal bias, 27
fear: authoritarianism using,
160; misinformation
causing false, 162–63;
misleading statements
causing, 165; public
education extremist views
causing, 162; right-wing
extremism weaponizing, 97
feelings and emotions, 152–53
Fiedler, Elizabeth, 129
First Amendment, 54
"flood the zone" tactics, 50
Floyd, George, 81
focus groups, 150
forced compliance, 37–38
Foster, Laura, 136–37

school board on students in, 130–33; superintendents approach to, 120–21
Liautaud, Susan, 95
librarians, 52, 110–12
Litman, Amanda, 137
Little Rock Central High School, 120
Little Rock Nine, 16
local elections, 46–48
Locke, R., 47
Louisville Independent School District, 84–87, 89–90, 92–93
love, 3
Luna, C., 47

Mann, Horace, 41
Marcotte, Amanda, 137
marginalized communities: advocacy for, 6; attacks on, 17; hatred toward, 21; school districts with, 81
Marvel Comics, 81–82
mass shootings, 21, 129
mathematics, 75–78
McCarthy, Joseph, 16–17
McCarthyism, 27–28, 58, 97
McMillan, James, 83
Meadows, Keely, 128
medical emergency, 9
melting pot, 37

Menzel, Scott: Horne's meeting with, 124–25; racist words of, 122; school board meetings supporting, 124; Superintendent of the Year award for, 124; as SUSD superintendent, 121; values and principles stated by, 123–24
middle school students, 77
middle school teachers, 75–76
Mikitarian, Elizabeth, 137
Milk, Harvey, 112–13
Miller, J., 61
misinformation, 104–5; false fears from, 162–63; from social media, 158, 165
misleading statements, 165
Miyares, Jason, 119
Moms for America, 53
Moms for Liberty, 134–35; candidates losing backed by, 114–15; as extremist group, 53, 116–17; Stop Moms for Liberty against, 137; Ziegler as founder of, 50
moral integrity, 62–63
moral strength, 32
Moss, Shaye Freeman, 46
*Murder and Extremism in the United States in 2022* (ADL), 46
*My Shadow Is Purple* (Stuart), 52

same-sex couples, 36
Sanders, Sarah Huckabee, 119
San Diego County, 45
Sarasota, Florida, 50
school board: critical race
theory banned by, 50;
extremist takeover of,
53–54; extremist views
in, 49–50; going against
superintendent, 91–92; on
LGBTQ+ students, 130–33;
like-minded people on, 79;
Pennridge School District
election for, 133–34; policies
protested of, 115–16;
politicization of, 48–50;
right-wing extremism
defeated and, 114–15; right-
wing extremism elected to,
49–50; voluntary integration
by, 86
school board meetings: arrests
and violence at, 26; group
norms for, 146; Menzel
supported by, 124; norms
set for, 145–46; Vitale
confronted in, 126
school board members: with
extremist views, 112–15,
120–28; Moms for Liberty
candidates losing to be,
114–15; students groomed
by, 127

school
districts: communications
of, 156–57; equity in, 71;
integrated systems in, 87,
93; with marginalized
people, 81; parents
protesting, 78; sex
discrimination in, 118;
student assignment plan in,
88–89
schools: academic subjects in,
101–2; bomb threats to,
52; charter, 49–50; cultural
wars involving, 127–28;
discriminatory attitudes
in, 36–37; diversity in, 37;
indoctrination manipulation
of, 53–57; instructional
material policies of, 36;
integration of, 82; officials
being threatened from, 49;
race isolated, 88; segregation
in, 93; students attending
desegregated, 83–84
Schwerner, Michael Henry, 19
Scottsdale Unified School
District (SUSD), 121–25
Second Red Scare, 18
See Our Truth (Education
Trust-New York), 72, 74
segregation, 5–6, 13, 28; in
Louisville Independent
School District, 89–90;
racism and, 93–94;

127; standing up for, 107;
transgender, 118, 127;
White and Black, 82–83
Superintendent of the Year,
71–72, 74, 124
superintendents: community
involved in hiring, 86–87;
LGBTQ+ approach of,
120–21; Menzel as SUSD,
121; school board going
against, 91–92
Supreme Court decisions,
83–84, 86
SUSD. *See* Scottsdale Unified
School District
*Swann v. Charlotte-
Mecklenburg Board of
Education* case, 83

taking action, risks of, 66–67
Teachers of the Year program,
51–52
Tea Party, 90
threats: authoritarianism using,
160; bomb, 52; intimidation
and, 98–99; in local
elections, 46–48; to school
officials, 49
transgender students, 118, 127
transgender youth, 119
*Trial Urban District
Assessment*, 89
tribalism, 105
truth, 22

two-way communications, 158

United States: Bill of Rights
in, 39–40; Constitution,
39–40; culture wars in,
19–20; Department of
Justice in, 49; discrimination
in, 16; divisiveness
in, 19–20; extremism
movement in, 23; founding
documents of, 15–16;
ideological divisions in, 1–2;
immigrants in, 37
Uridel, Louis, 125

validation, 154–55
values, in public education, 28
Vermilion, by extremist
group, 135
Vietnamese peasants, 61
violence, at school board
meetings, 26
Vitale, Julie, 125–28
voting rights, 23
Voting Rights Act (1965), 19
voucher system, 51

Walters, Ryan, 52
Wayne, John, 45, 58
well-being, of children, 66–67
Wenyuan Wu, 127
Wesley, Cynthia, 19
*White Fragility* (DiAngelo),
121–22

# ABOUT THE AUTHORS

**Sheldon Berman**, EdD, served as superintendent of four districts in three states—Hudson, Massachusetts; Jefferson County (Louisville), Kentucky; Eugene, Oregon; and Andover, Massachusetts—spanning twenty-eight school years. He provided leadership in state superintendent associations as well as in local and national education organizations. He served as Massachusetts Association of School Superintendents President and received the 2003 Massachusetts Superintendent of the Year Award and AASA's Distinguished Service Award in 2022, in addition to lifetime achievement awards for social-emotional learning and character education. He has made nationally significant contributions by furthering social-emotional learning practice, expanding special education funding and enhancing inclusive instructional strategies, advocating and implementing school integration, contributing guidance on administrative ethics through a decade of *School Administrator* "Ethical Educator" columns, and launching state-of-the-art virtual learning and instructional innovations. He has authored numerous book chapters, articles, policy reports, and op-eds, and has presented nationally and internationally on educational issues and innovations. He is the author of three books—*Implementing Social-Emotional Learning: Insights from Districts' Successes and Setbacks* (2023), *The Ethical Educator: Pointers and Pitfalls for School Administrators* (2022, with Joyce A. Barnes and David B. Rubin), and *Children's Social Consciousness and the Development of Social Responsibility* (1997)—and the coeditor of

*Promising Practices in Teaching Social Responsibility* (1993, with Phyllis LaFarge). Retired as a district superintendent, he is currently the AASA Lead Superintendent for Social-Emotional Learning and serves as a professor of practice at the University of Oregon, College of Education.

**Luvelle Brown**, EdD, is superintendent of the Ithaca City School District in Ithaca, New York. He also serves as an adjunct faculty member at SUNY Cortland and St. John Fisher College, both in New York. His recent work has been recognized through the 2022 AASA Effie H. Jones Humanitarian Award and the 2020 New York State Council of School Superintendents Appreciation Award. Other major accomplishments include being selected in 2017 as the New York State Superintendent of the Year and in 2021 to a seat on Learning 2025: National Commission on Student-Centered, Equity-Focused Education. A sought-after speaker for regional and national conferences, he was invited to be a featured speaker at President Barack Obama's National Superintendents' Summit at the White House in 2014. Active in professional organizations, he has served on the New York State Council of School Superintendents Executive Committee, the AASA Digital Consortium, the Center for Digital Education Advisory Council, and CoSN's EmpowerED Superintendents Advisory Panel. A prolific contributor to education journals and blogs, he is the author of the acclaimed 2018 book *Culture of Love: Cultivating a Positive and Transformational Organizational Culture*. His community involvement is reflected in his 2018 appointment to the Ithaca College Board of Trustees, his recognition as the 2019 Tompkins County (NY) Distinguished Citizen, and his role as cofounder of 100 Black Men of Central Virginia.

Made in United States
North Haven, CT
08 May 2024

52280646R00129